Lion Leadership

Lion Leadership

Lion Leadership

"When it comes to leadership
it's not the title that counts,
ask yourself,
am I worthy of following."
– Mike Rodriguez

Lion Leadership

LION
Leadership

MIKERODRIGUEZ

Tribute
Publishing
2016

Lion Leadership

Tribute
Publishing

Tribute Publishing

LION Leadership
First Edition September 2016

All Worldwide Rights Reserved
ISBN: 978-0-990-6001-9-0

Printed in the United States of America.

In God We Trust.

Lion Leadership

For all of those brave enough to lead.

Lion Leadership

CONTENTS

PROLOGUE

"Words of truth challenge strong minds and offend weak ones."

Leadership is a privilege. It requires courage and is not for the weak. Leadership is a responsibility of authority that should be earned and never given. Leadership is to be respected. Respect should not be groveled to subordinates in an effort to be earned. The proof of earned respect is displayed in the fact that the existing leaders made a decision to assign authority to the new leader based on qualifications, skill-set and capabilities.

Lion Leaders may not initially be liked. They should however, eventually be loved. This love can only come after time, after challenges, and after tests of endurance by all members of the team. This will only happen once the team knows that the Lion Leader always has their best interest at heart.

Lion Leaders create disruptive change when necessary. People do not like change and they will resist it. They will emotionally deflect and hide behind the false claims of their dislike for the leader. What they really dislike is the accountability to perform and the expectations to step outside of their mediocrity. Lion Leaders stretch comfort zones.

Whatever your current role is, know that you already have everything you need to start your journey towards success. By using the strategies contained in this book, you can effectively change the outcome of your results, and the results of others.

Join me as we challenge your current thoughts and ask you to embrace effective teamwork, proven strategies, and clarity of vision as you start your journey to become a Lion Leader.

- **Mike Rodriguez**

Lion Leadership

Lion Leadership

**"I am more afraid of
one hundred sheep led by a lion,
than one hundred lions led by a sheep."**
Charles Maurice de Talleyrand-Perigord

I

Are You out of Balance?

On any given day in certain areas of eastern or southern South Africa, you can find a pride of lions roaming the grasslands in search of food or resting in the shade provided by the Acacia trees. Their strategies for success are precise, driven by their natural instinct to survive. They live, hunt, and socialize within the infrastructure of their pride, which might have as many as 30 or more members. As a team, they are completely dependent on each other through a bond of trust and instinct. Each member plays a crucial role that contributes to the success of the pride.

Although you may not see or even identify with each role, the leader within the pride is established and very clear. With sizes that can go well over 500 lbs., the physical presence of the leader is unmistakable. It simply implies their authority.

Chapter I – Are You out of Balance?

For effective focus and balance, every pride must have a leader. Within the pride the leader has a position of dominance, but does not necessarily dominate to get results. The team acknowledges each role within the hierarchy and realizes that the leader of the pride is established to ensure their continued survival.

When a lion pride hunts, the female lions strategically set up the hunt. Their goal is to identify, pursue, and secure the prey. With discipline and precise focus, they will surround the target, but they are not there to kill. Their goal is only to isolate and trap the prey. Once they secure it, the pride leader appears, releasing his profound roar, and scares the prey into the direction of the waiting lionesses. The pride works together with precision, urgency, and optimal performance, utilizing each other's strengths. The lionesses, with low profiles, are the ones who approach the prey without being seen, since the leader's large mane would reveal its presence and compromise the mission. The lionesses are also much faster than the lion, and they are able to capture and contain the prey more efficiently.

Finally, as the hunt ends, the pride leader will enter the scene for the kill, using the strength of his mighty jaws and teeth. A pride works as a team and they get results. They are in balance. When we consider the structure of teams in today's market, we certainly do not want to replicate a pride hierarchy, however, there are key components of a pride infrastructure that we can certainly take note of and maybe even learn from. As leaders, we must strengthen our teams, by embracing the responsibility of our authority to lead effectively. We must become better.

The reason I am telling you this is because we are facing a major dilemma in our society today: leaders have lost their way and have become too soft. We have turned kindness into weakness and we have let compassion evolve into empathy. We are catering to the *wants* of our team members instead of holding strong to pursue the deep and necessary *needs* of the bigger cause for everyone. We have lost sight of the responsibility to help others to realize and see their potential and the vision; instead, we have negotiated with mediocrity and we are losing. The results show it. We have compromised our authority and we are out of balance.

My intent is not to insult, as I don't know you, but if these words hurt you, then maybe you should take an honest look at your leadership beliefs, style, approach, and results. I'm not saying that we don't have sharp, knowledgeable, and capable people leading today; I'm telling you that our world has changed and our leaders have incorrectly adjusted to operate from positions that have declined to weakness. We have gotten too soft and we are out of balance. We must realize this immediately and take massive action to make corrections, otherwise the ongoing decline might be irreversible.

Chapter I – Are You out of Balance?

My perspective on this matter is that the current generation has started a cause that is perpetuated through social media and validated by conversation. They have set out to determine and redefine leadership, based on their ideals, opinions, and wants, which are being driven by their own emotions. We are seeing narcissistic employees decide what they believe a good leader is or what a good leader should be. They have set new emotionally driven standards and we are accepting them, sometimes because they demand it. The issue with this matter is that it creates a major imbalance in teams, causing weakened leaders, ineffective organizations and compromised, vulnerable cultures in the workplace. Ironically, we have let the students tell the teachers how to teach. Sometimes we even apologize for our own actions that don't align with individual opinions. We have compromised the standards of performance based cultures and it is being exposed in our results.

Some of us have become lions being led by sheep.

I admit that I do understand why individuals have stepped up to share their skewed thoughts, concerns and opinions on leadership, no matter how misdirected they might be; they are crying out for us to become better. The challenge here is that they have falsely established the standards for 'better,' which is primarily based on their emotional needs. They have asked us to lower our standards, so they can feel better. The risk with accommodating these requests, is that weak leaders produce weak people and weaker results.

**"We are seeing narcissistic employees,
who might not have even led others before,
decide what they believe
a good leader is or should be."**

Emotion-Centric Employees

The ease of access to personal opinions and the great exposure to social media is growing the audience and the distorted cause. I call it an employee emotion-centric culture. In this type of culture, employees believe that the employer is responsible for making sure the culture is all about the employees, to the point of fault. On the surface, this may seem normal and acceptable, however, the risk is that the employee then becomes a *dependent* of the company, instead of an *asset*. Employees are an asset, but when an asset claims full benefit without full accountability, they become a lability and create more liabilities.

As an example, I recently saw an image posted on a popular social media outlet. It exposes the thought process of our new leadership culture being driven by the masses of emotion-centric employees. On the surface, the diagram and its contents seem relevant and true; the content gives people a warm fuzzy feeling. However, it is just another instance of the emotional-driven employee narcissism that is clearly creating an imbalance and weak leaders.

When you take a closer look, the diagram does not show or suggest ANY accountability on the part of the individual/employee.

- **The responsibility falls completely on the shoulders of the leader to provide for the employee.**
- **This model relieves the individual of any of their balanced share of the responsibility and accountability to perform.**

Yes, it is true that the variables listed on the diagram are needed and required, however, in its simplest form the diagram is clearly one-sided. From a deeper perspective, it is perpetuating an ideal of one-sided accountability that keeps cultures out of balance and creates pacified employees and weak leaders. The implications of this "me" mindset can be devastating if not corrected. Any reasonable individual using this philosophy in a *personal* relationship could clearly see that they would be out of balance, yet in the business world, we have incorrectly learned to accept this as a new standard.

In contrast, in a **Balanced Environment**, the Lion Leader assumes authority. They use the core values listed in the previous diagram, but they partner them (NOT replace them) with these necessary and equal values:

OUR EMPLOYEES CAN STAY WHEN THEY

MikeRodriguezInternational.com

CREATE VALUE   SEEK MENTORS   ACCEPT CHALLENGES   ARE PROMOTABLE   STAY INVOLVED

SHOW
APPRECIATION   VALUE
OTHERS   SUPPORT
THE MISSION   EMPOWER
THEMSELVES   ARE
TRUSTWORTHY

This approach creates a strategic balance of accountability for each party. I call it a **Balanced Environment.**

In this model, the employer has a responsibility to develop the employee, but the employee also has an equal and important responsibility to perform: 100% pay for 100% performance. Accountability is held at the individual level, by the individual, and managed up through the levels of authority. Extra value is given only when the employee

7

demonstrates the ability to show value, above and beyond the standards of their position. Team members are respected, coached, and developed together. They are given the autonomy and freedom to perform to the established standards, however, they are equally expected to be accountable for their performance, regardless of the outcome.

In a balanced environment everyone is responsible for his/her own actions and has an expectation to succeed, fail, and grow as a team. Everyone works toward the vision as a critical part, not as individuals or segmented teams with personal agendas. Every person understands that their individual actions affect the team, which in turn affects the entire organization.

As a leader, you need to evaluate your environment to determine your current situation. Be honest as you answer these questions:

- **Have you compromised or maybe even lost your authority?**
- **Has your team set the standard for the direction and culture?**
- **Are you operating from a position of weakness?**
- **Have you become too soft?**
- **Are you accepting mediocrity?**

Chapter I – Are You out of Balance?

If you answered yes to any of these, then you need to reevaluate and reengage as a Lion Leader using the strategies in this book. Please know that it is never too late to change your mind about changing your direction.

At this point if you are completely confused and disconnected, then you are managing by emotions and not logic. Emotional people react, deflect and defend their opinions. Lion Leaders evaluate and protect the best interest of the team. The concepts that I am sharing are meant to challenge you and, as a result, you will feel very uncomfortable. However, a Lion Leader realizes that in order to be effective, you must be willing to be uncomfortable and not let your feelings overtake you.

So have we as leaders, failed our teams? I believe we have. Some of us have incorrectly led with a heavy hand. We abused our authority and we've pushed people too far. As a result, our teams lost sight of the vision and they lost confidence in us. They may have even confused "the" vision as "our own" vision and simply became unwilling to follow either one. This authoritative mindset is still happening today. Some leaders ridiculously rest on the false belief that leadership is based on having a title or a position. These are egotistical and self-centered people who create more damage in the workplace than they are even worth. The belief that having a title makes you a great leader is about as ridiculous as believing that baking a frozen pizza makes you a master chef; it's an insult.

Then we have those who believe that leading primarily from a position of kindness and love is the answer. They have abused the concept of kindness and, as a result, they have disastrous results. "My staff loves me" they emotionally claim, all while the truth reveals itself in the lack of respect for discipline and performance in the office.

**There is no glory in lowering yourself
to make others feel better.
The true test is being courageous enough
to help others rise to become better.**

What is Lion Leadership?
When we talk about true, bold leadership, which I call Lion Leadership, I am going to challenge you and your existing beliefs. My goal is not to tell you what you want to hear, but to tell you what you need to hear. Some of the information contained in this book will cause you to feel uncomfortable and you will want to question it. That's okay, that is my goal. You can only grow when you get uncomfortable when you are challenged.

Lion Leadership starts with having confidence in who you are and in your role. As a definition, confidence is the belief in yourself and your abilities to serve others. In contrast, arrogance is a belief in yourself and your abilities to serve yourself. So yes, confidence does belong in leadership, it is necessary. It is the representation of your self-esteem and the importance in your role. Why? Because to whom much is given, much is expected and you cannot give much if you don't have much to give. Every leader is important and every leader should start by believing in who they are. The team needs this from the leader and the company should expect this from every leader as well. However, the leader also has a responsibility to keep this in balance.

Today, if someone is confident as a leader, the masses take issue. They start to criticize the person with the intent to bring the person down to what they feel is a manageable level. They do this by packaging up their claim and criticizing or shaming the person, in an attempt to tone the person down. This approach is wrong and is usually driven by the insecurities of the crowd, who dislike the accountability and the level of authority.

A weak leader will cave in easily to appease the masses and, unfortunately, will compromise their role as a leader, as they forfeit their authority. Lion Leaders do not lower themselves to make others feel better. Lion Leaders challenge and inspire others to rise to become better! Your team needs to know that you believe in yourself, your company, your goals and in them! They need to know so they can believe in you and eventually in who they are, so they can become more. They also need to know where they stand with you, so they can grow.

Your ability to have confidence in yourself as a leader, will be one of the most important driving forces that you possess.

Lion Leaders ALWAYS lead from a position of strength. This means that even when you are wrong, you need to apologize, but do not come across as weak. In other words, you can genuinely apologize for 'an action' without comprising 'your position' as a leader. When you make a mistake and you apologize, this is actually the most critical time that they need you to be humbled and strong.

This is how trust is validated. However, I must point out very clearly that you are never to apologize if you have not done anything wrong. We live in a very sensitive and emotionally-driven society today. Some individuals are looking for things to complain about and looking for ways for you to buy into their complaints! Some of them even genuinely believe that you have wronged them or that you are in the wrong even when you aren't. The goal in these situations is to listen to their words and to understand the person. When you react and apologize for who you are, you are validating the person's emotional position and comprising your position as leader.

When people begin to say things with 'I feel, I think, or I believe,' these are called emotional drivers, meaning that emotions are driving their actions, not their logic or data.

People use emotional drivers when they lack facts or when they are overwhelmed in an attempt to dominate you emotionally, manipulate you, or simply to justify their cause. (This will be covered later in Facts vs. Opinions.) For example, an employee might say, "I **feel** you were a bit tough on us today when you asked us not to be late to team meetings." The big issue here really is why were they late in the first place, but as we know, emotionally driven employees like to deflect accountability back on other people; in this case it will be deflected to you. Be cool and calm. Your response:

"I'm very sorry you feel that way. Can you please tell me what I said or did that you feel was tough?"

After you ask, please be quiet and respectfully wait for an answer. Do not give answers as options for them. This approach prevents you from being drawn into an emotional conversation and puts the accountability back on the person for their concerns to be validated with data. You are asking them to shift from emotions to facts. This method also keeps them engaged and streamlined, to only deal with the facts (the data), and pulls them away from their emotional drivers, so you can focus on the real issue: their tardiness. This is important because a Lion Leader always operates from a position of calm control and only deals with the facts. We will listen to opinions, but we only make decisions based on facts.

In these types of situations, the employee's answer will usually reinforce how 'they feel' or they will attempt to take you down a path that highlights 'you' as the issue and not their actual behavior of being late. In fact, most of their answers wont address the facts. They might answer you by saying, "Well, other people are late," (deflecting) or "It hurt my feelings" (emotion) or "I don't think you are treating me fairly" (opinion). Either way, you simply address their answer by bringing them back to the facts: their tardiness. You would say:

"I can understand how you feel; so do you think it's okay for you to be late?"

In this situation they will only have two ways to answer your question:
- **yes**
- **no**

If they answer No, then you are now in balance and you have common ground. If they say Yes, you simply respond and ask "Please tell me why you think it's okay to be late?" Once again, you have thrown accountability back to them to justify their behavior with facts, not emotion. Either way, you will be at a point where you can move towards resolution.

Chapter I – Are You out of Balance?

Remember that a Lion Leader shows respect always, even when being disrespected. We do this because we know that the person who is launching the verbal assault is emotionally out of balance. We stay in control and we also know that through our confidence, we always work to stay in balance. We will listen, hear, and respond with facts, not emotion, and we ask questions for clarification to get to common ground. We do this because it is our responsibility to work towards resolution and because others are watching us, which affects how they interact with us. It is also our responsibility to be confident as a leader. You will have many opportunities to teach when you are challenged. The most effective way to teach is through your actions, not your words. Here are a highlights to remember:

Lion Leaders are patient.
We expect results and will not tolerate complacency. Through this we teach others not to accept complacency. However, we know that true results take time while we develop the skill and the person. We know that a person who is addressed with patience will learn to focus and have discipline and patience.

Lion Leaders are humble and kind.
We recognize that giving a smile and nice words are not gestures of weakness. Our words and actions are a representation of our love for our work and for our team. However, we have learned not to display our kindness in a way that can be confused as weakness.

15

Lion Leaders are passionate.
How can your team operate with passion when the leader isn't passionate? We stand firm on our tough decisions that are beneficial for the team, even when the team doesn't understand. However, we are willing to modify plans when it is necessary for the betterment of the team.

Lion Leaders responsibly manage their authority.
We don't push people; we pull them into their greatness. If they choose not to come, we help them to find their way out. We never abuse our authority or violate company codes of conduct.

**Some will confuse your confidence as arrogance.
Know who you are.**

Your Authority

I once was told by someone with passion and confidence that "Leadership is action, not position." After becoming a leader, I quickly determined that this was simply not true. I have seen many unqualified people with impressive titles who took decisive, unskilled action to ineffectively lead people and organizations to their demise.

Lion Leadership is responsibly handling your authority to help your team exceed the expected results. Read that sentence again, and please don't add, change, or remove words. Authority is a power granted to you. So as a leader you automatically carry authority. The people who granted it to you trusted that you are capable of managing it. If you started your own business, then you responsibly assigned that authority to yourself. Either way, as a Lion leader, you must accept and embrace your authority. You never abuse it and you never compromise it either. Early in my career, I was fortunate enough to have a boss who was a prime example of a Lion Leader. He talked with the staff in a kind and respectful manner. He laughed at funny jokes and smiled to let you know that he appreciated you. However, when it came time to perform and focus on results, it was very clear where you stood with him. It was also clear that he had our best interest at heart. Even if you had just been joking with him in the hall, once the meeting started or staff involvement was needed, we knew that we needed to pay attention and get serious. When he talked, we listened.

Chapter I – Are You out of Balance?

When he called one of us in to review a deficiency, we listened. We listened because he knew his authority. He used it wisely and responsibly and therefore we respected it and him. We did not fear him. We were all focused and committed to the vision established by our leader.

As a leader, you are displaying your authority in every task and encounter that you make. Just as a lion has no reason to run around roaring, you have no good reason to run around barking orders. That is an abuse of your authority. True power is displayed through disciplined and balanced behavior. Your staff knows that you carry the title and they know you have the power; you don't need to remind them. However, when they see you issuing encouragement when it is called for, and disciplining, and making tough decisions as you stand by them, then they witness your authority firsthand. That is how boundaries of respect are built.

Leading vs. Managing – The Red String

Anyone can manage; it takes desire, skill, courage, discipline, and heart to be a leader.

I remember applying for my first management job. I was excited to start implementing my policy, defining my rules, pushing my agendas, and getting people to get things done. My plan was to make people work as hard as I did to excel. I was so naïve and was operating from a selfish mentality. I was far from being a Lion Leader.

Chapter I – Are You out of Balance?

I recall going to lunch with the vice president and one of the owners for my first interview. In my mind, my confidence was going to make up for my lack of experience. I was ready for the interview and prepared to answer the toughest questions, or so I thought. As we sat down at the table and the VP introduced me, the owner calmly and confidently delivered the first question: "Have you led people before?" My answer was a confident "no" followed by my attempt to explain my strengths. He wasn't buying. He reached into his pocket and pulled out a red string.

After carefully laying the string on the table, he looked at me and began to share a simple but profound concept. He placed one of his fingers on one end of the string and began to push the string. As he pushed it on the table, he asked me, "What happens to the string as I push it?" I looked down at the string, noticing that it was going all over the place. I told him that the string seems to be going everywhere. He smiled. Then with his same finger on the end of the string, he began to pull the string in the opposite direction. He pulled it all around the table top, making circles and all sorts designs. He looked at me and asked me a question that would change my way of thinking: "What happens as I pull the string?" I answered, "It goes wherever you take it." "Yes," he said. "That's it." He smiled at me.

Leading people is the same concept. When you push people they will go everywhere and nowhere at the same time. When you lead, they will follow you and everything can

19

become streamlined. Pushing people causes resistance and creates stress for both of you. Pulling involves coaching, encouragement, and not tolerating less than their best. I got the concept, although it would take me many years to master.

When we talk about differences between leading and managing, some people see this as a semantic, but it isn't. There are very distinct differences between the two. Managing is how you work with tasks, projects, and reports. Leadership is how you work with people.

Managers and leaders have very different attitudes towards people and tasks:

Managers vs.	Leaders
- Focus on Tasks	- Focus on Skill
- Direct People	- Coach People
- Focus on Process	- Focus on Results
- Are about Themselves	- Are About Others

You don't mange people,
you manage things.
You lead people.

Leadership Styles

Once you can acknowledge and understand that there are distinct differences between managing and leading, the next step is to identify your leadership style so you can make the necessary adjustments.

As I work with leadership around the world, I have determined that there are four core leadership styles that people have a tendency to operate within. These styles are typically amplified during periods of stress, causing us to see the worst, or in some cases, the best in a person. Most of us in early stages of our career will emulate a previous style of a manager that we believed to be effective.

We also will eliminate styles that we believe were ineffective. The challenge with this 'adaptive strategy,' is that you will have a tendency to work within a silo, too focused on the style, neglecting your effectiveness and your results. Take into consideration that Lion Leaders ALWAYS lead from a position of disciplined strength. We balance our personality and emphasize our strengths to get the best results.

The Buddy Leader –

At some point we have all worked with someone who fits this category. They are the boss that everyone loves (or so the Buddy Leader thinks). Ironically, the Buddy Leader doesn't see himself as the boss. A Buddy Leader takes the approach that they are everyone's friend and that their job is to ensure a happy and friendly work environment. Their goal is simply unrealistic as conflict is a requirement for growth. This person has usually adopted this weak strategy as a result of a bad experience with a former boss or just as an attempt to be liked by everyone. This style is more of a coping mechanism than a leadership style, because no one is really being led.

I have met a few Buddy Leaders in my life who were liked by their entire team, however, their ineffective strategy always came with a cost. The Buddy Leader lacks authority and vision. When you are too nice to too many people too much of the time, it becomes very difficult for staff to take you seriously when you need to address serious business matters. We find that acts of discipline are often laughed at or even overlooked altogether. No one takes a Buddy Leader seriously when seriousness is required.

The benefit - people will like you, but it will come with a big cost.

The risks - you will lose your authority and sometimes respect as a leader. Eventually, the Buddy Leader loses all credibility during times of required discipline, crisis, or sometimes during standard daily accountability with people.

How you can tell if you have Buddy Leader tendencies:

- **Do you frequently take action to please everyone regardless of the impact on the business?**

- Do you deflect and blame others for a change in policy or for a reprimand that must be carried out?
- Do you compromise business policy to allow yourself to look good?
- Do you find that your staff doesn't take you serious during business impacting moments?

If you answered yes to any of these, then you should take a closer look at your style and take massive action to address your weak areas.

The Authoritative Leader –

In contrast to the Buddy Leader, who wants to be everyone's friend, the Authoritative Leader is often too overbearing or demanding in enforcing policy and results. The Authoritative Leader often assumes an autocratic role with their position, overlooking the important team aspect of the organization. They adopt an 'It's about ME, not us,' mentality. These leaders put too much emphasis on the authority they have been given and little to no attention on the team's needs. Simply stated, they are title driven, thinking too much about who they are and the power they have been given in their role. This type of leader is usually disconnected from their staff, although they usually aren't aware of it, or if they are, they typically don't care. Authoritative Leaders distortedly view the work environment as "me against them" while ensuring that everyone is aware of the leader's title and position.

The benefit - Often perceived as egomaniacs, these type of leaders often get the results they desire. However, the results will come at the expense of compromising the team's morale.

The risks - Expect high turnover, a lack of team bonding, fear misinterpreted as respect, and an increase in HR complaints in an environment with an authoritative type.

How you can tell if you have Authoritative Leader tendencies:

- **Do you frequently take action without getting additional team input?**
- **Do you oversee multiple tasks dictating the process and overseeing the results of the staff?**
- **Do you disregard business policy to allow your personal agenda?**
- **Do you find that your staff limits communication with you or just agrees with you on most things?**

If you answered yes to any of these, then you should take a closer look at your style and take massive action to address your weak areas.

The Detailed Leader –
There is nothing wrong with being conscious of reports, numbers, and other details, as they are important. However, when these things take priority over your staff, how you communicate with them, and your team involvement, then your detailed management style has become a liability. I have worked with Detailed Leaders who ensure that all aspects of the work reporting and metrics are being completed. They are focused on analytics, reports, and deadlines, in tune with the all of the details. The challenge is that this focus comes at the expense of the team, who is often overlooked with the necessary human interaction. If you are spending too much time with reports, numbers, or playing in your CRM, then you should consider this your wake up call.

The benefit – Data is good, too much data isn't. Numbers, forecasts, metrics, and percentages are almost always spot on. They can give you the reports you need, when you need them, and most information is precise.

The risks – Too much data means too little human interaction. Expect a low interacting team, moderate morale, and increased stress at the end of the month or quarter when they are compiling data from their team.

The Lion Leader (The Balanced Leader)
The Lion Leader is a balanced leader who recognizes their authority, but does not abuse it with an authoritative approach. They have adopted the strengths from each of the other three styles, while eliminating the risky tendencies. They don't have to be authoritative, because they have earned the respect of the team. They do this by doing what they say they are going to do and they lead by example. Although a Lion Leader is friendly to the staff, they also keep the established boundaries intact by recognizing and respecting actions and behaviors in the workplace. A Lion Leader doesn't cross the line with their authority or with careless actions. They are friendly without comprising respect or their ability to manage disciplinary situations. They focus on reports and numbers, but never let numbers become the priority over individual results. Instead they see details as a requirement to report excellent performance.

Benefits of being a Lion Leader – Your team knows where they stand. Lion Leaders operate from a position of disciplined and silent strength. They can earn the respect of the team by being genuine with communication, involved when necessary, confident with business matters, and fair during challenging team situations.

The risks – None, because Lion Leaders are:

- **Responsible**
- **Fair**

- **Respected**
- **Wise users of their authority**
- **They get results, because they work to stay in balance.**

You already possess all of the courage you need. Claim it and rise to defeat your challenge.

Your Belief System

I challenge you to take an open and honest approach as you evaluate your current management style. Consider your tendencies and identify your strengths and weaknesses. The goal is not for you to change who you are as a person, the goal is for you to make the appropriate modifications to your words, thoughts, and actions. You do this to ensure that you get the best possible results with your team morale, your team deficiencies, team planning, and overall performance. Understand that as a leader, you won't be able to take the appropriate action to change unless you believe you can. As I talk with and train leadership and teams around the world, I have determined that the most important contributing factor that impacts your ability to make changes in your life, is your belief system.

In life and in work, your belief system determines how you see yourself, how you see others, and it ultimately affects the decisions you make and actions you take to get your results.

The concept itself is very simple: what you believe is what you will follow. Therefore, you will not follow or take action on something that you don't believe in. For example, as you are reading this book, if you don't believe that the principles and strategies that I am sharing will work for you, then they won't. You won't let them. It's basic human nature. You won't act on what you don't believe in. This is true with all aspects of life and business.

The answer: Challenge your belief system! Ask yourself:

- **Who you think you are versus who you should be as a Leader.**

- **Do you believe that you are capable of achieving more and becoming the leader that you and your team deserves?**

- **If so, then own it and take action!**

Take a look at this diagram that I created. I use it to illustrate how our beliefs create the foundations that help us to build our desired results.

MIKERODRIGUEZ
© 2016

1. What you believe affects your thoughts
2. Your thoughts in turn influence your attitude
3. Your attitude will be a contributing factor to
4. Your decisions and if you decide to take the appropriate action
5. Your actions will ultimately determine
6. Your results

With a negative belief system, this will be a vicious circle, because getting 'no results' or even 'poor results' will reinforce your beliefs in a negative way. If you don't change, you will continue the process every day of your life, causing you to generate the same results again and again. Our goal is to create a system of positive beliefs in order to get the desired positive results. So, if you believe that you are capable of being a Lion Leader, then you will think of ways to become better and you will use these strategies.

Once you think about positive solutions and improved results, your attitude will improve to reflect your thoughts. Your positive or good attitude will now allow you to make the best decisions that are aligned with your thoughts, prompting you to take the appropriate actions decisively and confidently.
The actions you take will generate either:

- **a positive result (a win) or**
- **a negative result (a loss)**

Either outcome is fine, because the results are a direct reflection of your actions and that you believe in what you are doing. If you win, then you rinse and repeat. If you experience a loss, you simply look at it as a learning experience. Lion Leaders never take failure personally. We know that failure is an equal and necessary part of success. We consider failure an opportunity to re-evaluate.

**Lion Leaders understand that
failure isn't who we are.
Failure is a result of something that
we did or did not do.**

In a scenario where someone has adopted a positive belief system, you can easily see how their thoughts, attitudes, decisions, actions, and results will simply follow each other to reinforce their beliefs.

By evaluating your belief system in all areas of your life, you can start to understand who you are and who you are not. What you believe is inevitably what you will live and what you will achieve.

Belief is the obstacle that can prevent us from taking action, or it can influence and ignite our actions. It all works together like a complex puzzle, yet it can be managed...if you only believe. The truth is that you will only become what you believe.

Chapter I – Are You out of Balance?

Chapter I – Are You out of Balance?

What do YOU believe?

Chapter II – Understanding Team Culture

**"A lion never loses sleep
over the opinions of sheep."**
Unknown

II

Understanding Team Culture

Times have changed, people have changed, and standards are changing. Someone needs to take action to ensure long term success and health of the organization. That person should be the leader or someone who steps up to lead.

Some leaders have become afraid of what people think. Lion Leaders don't care what you think. They recognize that opinions are usually misrepresented recommendations fueled by emotion and clouded with insult. Lion Leaders aren't afraid to take a stand and uphold boundaries that protect the best interest of the organization, not the agenda of a few. They do this by being as bold as a lion. They challenge their team to share ideas to become better; they challenge the ideas and encourage the team to challenge each other. They do this to stay ahead, aligned with progress and for the survival of the organization, because there is not a 'constant standard' in today's marketplace. Lion Leaders recognize what worked in the past might not have the same impact today, or it might not even be relevant. In order to grow as leaders, we must embrace change. Lion Leaders vet through opportunities of change, removing opinions and emotion. They know that change is difficult for people to embrace, not because change is bad, but because it makes people uncomfortable. Since we can agree that most people operate within their comfort levels, it goes without saying that a culture will be defined by the team's ability to successfully change. This, of course, depends on a leader's ability to lead.

It is natural for people to resist change and to only focus on the negative aspects. A Lion Leader sees and understands this. They challenge the staff to not only confront the difficulty associated with change, but also realize the benefits and help to guide the team through. When a team can work together towards a goal, the culture will improve, regardless if they fail or succeed. If a team, working together, encounters failure, they understand that it is only temporary and they re-engage to find a new way. An aligned team that accomplishes success is creating a bond and reinforcing their vision. Every business has created their own culture based on the accepted mindset of everyone's ability to deal with change.

In a **Healthy Culture**, there is balance. Leadership has validated their trust and the team works together to uphold the standards and the results. The team can see and understand the vision, which impacts their morale and their quality of work. They know the boundaries and respect them.

In a **Broken Culture**, it's just the opposite. The team is out of balance because trust has been compromised somewhere along the way. Team attitudes are severely influenced by individual attitudes. Bad attitudes are validated as others act poorly together and the team slowly accepts the behavior. The end result is that no one is performing or they are performing at less than desirable levels. A Lion Leader's job is to establish the culture for the benefit of all.

In any team culture, we find that it is either:
- **fashionable to be positive and perform, or**
- **it is acceptable not to**

My research has determined that a culture can decline and become complacent very quickly due to poor performance or negative attitudes. In fact, years ago I conducted an experiment with a team to validate this fact. I have outlined the study on the next few pages, using two different scenarios.

Scenario number 1-

I gathered together seven people in a conference room and asked them to pretend that they were a fictitious team of seven people. I assigned different names and roles to each person. Of the seven people, six were told that they were at 100% or above the established performance levels and only one of them, Joe, was to be at less than 50% of his performance levels. Next, I went around the conference table to each of the six people in the room, with Joe present, and asked them to give their thoughts on Joe's results. This what they said:

- Joe is dragging down the team.
- Joe needs to step it up.
- What is Joe doing all day?
- Joe should probably consider quitting.
- Some said Joe should be fired.
- They held Joe personally accountable for his results.

After I gathered everyone's input, I asked Joe, based on the teams input, what he thought of his performance, relative to the team's performance. I also asked how he felt about their input. This is what he said:

- I feel terrible.
- I'm not carrying my workload.
- I'm holding everyone back.
- I really feel like I should quit.

Based on this fictitious scenario, everyone had proudly spoken up about Joe to ensure the high levels of the fictitious performance standards were being kept. This caused them to resent Joe and caused Joe to feel inadequate. Joe didn't feel that he was contributing to the team and others wanted him to feel the pain of not doing his part.

Scenario Number 2 –

Once again, I asked everyone to pretend that they were a fictitious team of seven, but this time I assigned the same six people new performance levels. I went around the table, let each person know their new results, which varied, but now had changed and were at or below **50%** of their required fictitious performance levels. **Please note that I informed "Joe" that he was still at 50% or less of required performance levels.**

Under these *new* circumstances, with lower performance levels across the board, when I went around the table and asked the six people in the room, with Joe present, to give their thoughts on Joe's results, this is what they said:

- Joe needs help with his performance.
- Joe was working hard but the results weren't there.
- We should cut Joe some slack.
- Now, they said Joe should not quit.
- They said Joe should not be fired.
- They blamed the company for Joe's failure.

After I gathered everyone's input on Joe, I asked Joe what he thought of his performance relative to the team's performance and what he felt about their input. This is what he said:

- Man I feel good and accepted.
- I'm right in line with everybody else.
- The company is letting me down.

The end result of the experiment was that in both of scenarios, Joe's circumstances stayed exactly the same. It never changed. However, his mindset about his performance changed as the team changed their perspective. In his mind he adjusted to the culture.

In scenario 1:
- Everyone was "performing" and Joe felt bad.
- Joe wanted to quit because he let the team down.
- Everyone wanted Joe to step it up or quit.
- Joe wasn't upholding the team standards.
- Joe felt personally accountable.

In scenario 2:
- Everyone was under-producing just like Joe.
- Everyone felt right in line with Joe.
- They even felt bad for Joe.

- Now Joe no longer felt he needed to quit, even though HIS circumstances had never changed.
- Joe now blamed the company.

This experiment proves two things:

1. When the majority of your staff **is not** producing, the culture is accepted as one of non-performance. Everyone feels okay, even though no one is actually doing their job. This creates a culture of complacency and blame and will eventually lead to less results with less accountability.
   RESULT: The culture is broken and will continue to decline.

2. When the majority of your staff is producing, everyone takes pride in what they are doing together and the team will defend the high standards. Everyone feels great about their performance and non-performance is not tolerated or accepted. People hold each other accountable.
   RESULT: The culture is healthy and performance-based and will continue to grow.

**Your team culture is created
by the way you think, act, interact, and
by what you accept from your team.**

Set higher standards and hold people accountable.

As a Lion Leader, ask yourself these questions:
- Are you contributing to a broken culture by tolerating low or mediocre performance?
- Are you engaged with your team to see who or what is breaking your culture?
- Do you notice staff who are comfortable or resentful with others who are not performing to team or company standards?

If so, it's time to take action. You start by bringing disruptive change to your team to improve your culture. This creates an incentive for people to move up or to move out. Before you react with an opinion on that statement, remember that a Lion Leader recognizes and owns the responsibility to perform. This means that if people need help, you help them. Those who don't want to participate have already told you that they don't want to be on board by their actions. Stay strong, stay focused, and don't let your emotions cloud your vision. The goal is not to run people off. The point is that when you give people choices and options to improve and they don't take them, they have already made and have given you their decision.

The real question is why are you paying and keeping someone around who doesn't want to be there?

Three Types of Employees

When I started my professional career, I was fortunate to be hired by an organization that had established a healthy team culture of performance. Although most people around me were performing, I wasn't a performer and I could feel that I was dragging the team down. I felt terrible. I quickly realized that if I wanted my results to change, then I needed to change. I considered myself capable and smart, I just wasn't working with my true potential. I had developed a bad habit of hanging around with a few individuals who also weren't performing, and I noticed that they complained quite a bit. They had an excuse for everything and their blame, attitudes and belief systems were out of control. I no longer wanted to be part of their group, so I took action to break away.

Over the next few years I would study this phenomenon. As a result, I created categories for stages of employee growth to help monitor my pace and the pace of teams I worked with. Now, years later with decades of experience, I have formalized this study for leaders to easily identify and determine where people rank in their minds. The mind, of course, is what drives the actions, based on beliefs.

My research has concluded that there are three core types of people in life and/or employees in the workplace:

1. The Complainers

This group makes up about 22% of people, yet they create the biggest damage. Their bad attitudes and low to no performance not only jeopardize their careers, but they also create negative effects on the organization. These are the people who show up to work (and life) because they have to. Something has happened in their lives that has prompted them to lose their focus, their passion, and/or their drive. They aren't happy with some facet of their life, (it might be their job) and they let everyone know, either verbally or through their lack of involvement. These people are disappointing in many ways, but primarily because they show up to work, expecting 100% of their paycheck every pay period, while refusing to give 100% effort in return. The core of their foundation is that they don't believe that much is happening or will happen in their lives, but they believe they are owed much. Ironically, they create their own demise through self-destructive behavior.

Complainers are highly deficient in personal accountability and detrimental to the overall health of the organization. They come to work late, gossip, conduct personal tasks during business hours, have extended lunch hours, and they leave work early. Nothing is ever their fault and they typically lead a life of blame. Most company cultures are impacted heavily by the complainers, especially when they see more and more complainers develop within the organization. If you have ever worked at a company where people were telling you all of the bad things about the employer, peers, product, and everything else they could find wrong, then you were working with complainers. Their disease is highly contagious and their behavior should be addressed quickly with decisive action. Complainers are culture changers, negative impactors, and creators of resistance. Their poor attitudes not only affect their overall performance, but they will also hold back the progress of the entire team if you don't Lead them like a Lion.

The goal isn't to terminate the complainer, the goal is to get them to recognize their unacceptable behavior and to give them the opportunity to take immediate and planned action to correct it. Remember, any manager can fire someone, but a Lion Leader accepts every challenge to develop all employees and turn them around. Again, if any employee isn't willing to improve, then they have already made their decision. A Lion Leader learns this quickly and acts on it. When this happens, you must help the person to exit your organization with a legal, ethical, and soundproof plan. You do this for their own happiness and for the health and culture of your organization.

The good news is that most complainers are indeed aware that they are complainers. They are normally not called out for their behavior, especially in today's market, so when they are confronted, they will usually respond by either:

a. **getting back on board to win or**
b. **planning their exit strategy**

Either way is a win-win for both of you, but ultimately your goal is to get them to move up to the next level of performance and accountability. I have seen many complainers who stay with organizations for years, because they are never called out for their behavior (poor leadership). I have seen many leave the organization and take their poor behavior somewhere else. Finally, I have seen a few complainers in my career who take responsibility for their actions and they take action to improve (Lion Leadership). This group will always need the guidance and mentorship of a fair, caring, and true Lion Leader who does not negotiate with mediocrity.

2. The Complacent

This group accounts for approximately 68% of people. Complacent people are the ones who show up and do their job. They usually won't do any more, unless asked. These are the typical people who have fallen into the daily routines of their lives. They have confused the fact that because they are doing something and they are getting a result, that everything is fine. They live and operate from a perspective that as long as they are comfortable, all is okay. This simply isn't true, because when most complacent people increase their attitudes and action, we find that they can achieve more out of work and life. The problem is that people in this group are comfortable and they don't want to get uncomfortable, which is a requirement for change. They are indeed capable of producing much more, if they can only find a reason to take action. They are missing out on a much better quality of life and they aren't giving the company the best that either of them deserves. Complacent people should be encouraged and challenged to become all that they are capable of. Lion Leaders help them find their reason to excel and help them grow to the next level.

3. The Competitors

This third group is unique and accounts for less than 10% of people, but they have the greatest impact on culture. I have found that almost every person in this group has been a complainer or has been complacent at some point in their life or career. They have experienced the same pains, failures, and personal challenges, yet what makes this group different is that they have made a decision to overcome these common obstacles to achieve more. **They show up to win.** They have taken personal responsibility and taken action to make their lives better. They understand that by being a better employee, the organization and the people they work with become better as well.

Competitor's show up to win and they want others to win. They also recognize that winning is a decision. They have purpose, they see the company vision, and they take accountability. They have developed the core qualities to become a Lion Leader and you will find your leadership candidates in this group.

However, know that there are two types of competitors:

a. **Reckless Competitor**

These individuals are driven, but they are all about themselves. They will usually do or say whatever is necessary to get the end result to succeed, sometimes at any cost. This group won't usually be part of the team, but they can and sometimes do make the transition to become a:

b. **Balanced Competitor**

People who operate with integrity, passion, teamwork, strategy, and vision. They see the big picture and follow a plan to win.

Regardless of where you are as a leader, or where members of your team may be in any of these three categories, know that anyone can change if they choose to. They just need to know that you will support them, and they need to feel part of the team and part of the vision. This doesn't mean you compromise and lighten up on accountability. This is a living process and you will see each member of your team go through different stages, falling into and moving out of each of the three categories, based on their beliefs and attitudes. Your job as a leader is to stay engaged and be present to keep your team engaged. When people see that you have their best interest at heart, that you believe in them and that you have high expectations for them, they will surprise you with their willingness to change.

Snowballs in Your Organization

Regardless of what category you or members of your team might be in, there is a constant struggle to stay at the Competitor Level. Certain factors can create catalysts: life events, attitude, work challenges, and other matters that prompt people to slow down or speed up their performance. In the business world today, we are managing and leading ineffectively. Many are reactive 'managers,' not leaders, and are simply going through the motions each day. Part of the standard process that most organizations have adopted today is to onboard, train on product, and then wait and see if the employees perform. They limit interaction and involvement with the staff to the point of disconnecting with the people. Then, when they do notice big issues, it's usually too late. People get emotionally involved, react to the negative results by putting the employee on plan, and then manage them out the door.

As a Lion Leader, one of your key objectives is to always keep an eye out for problem areas and manage through them before they get out of control. I call these snowballs. If you place a small snowball at the top of a hill and slowly roll it to the bottom, of course it gets much larger along the way and becomes more difficult to handle. It's the same with problem areas pertaining to people and situations at work. If we don't notice and address them when they are small, they will become more difficult to address as time goes by. Eventually they will become too big to effectively deal with or even resolve.

I have seen organizations who have snowballs with tardiness, performance, and even attitudes. I'll meet with leaders who will tell me they have a problem with an employee. When I asked the leader when the problem started, they didn't know. All they know is they have this giant snowball that they need help removing. My point to them is that they should have caught it earlier and not let it get to this point.

Lion Leaders don't like snow, so when they see a snowball, he or she immediately must turn on the radar to determine:
- **What** the snowball is
- **Why** it's happening
- **When** it started
- **How** it can be melted (eliminated)

As an example, I am going to use tardiness, but you can use any issue in place of tardiness to practice:

Tom is a complacent employee, but he always shows up to work on time. However, you have noticed that this is the second Friday in a row that Tom has come to work 45 minutes late. You now have a snowball. (Not yet a problem, but outside of standard operations for Tom.)

What:
A potential trend with consistent tardiness.

Facts:
- It happens on Fridays.
- This is the second time (the details, such as the times/dates of each tardiness should be known).
- Tom is normally consistently on time.

Remember, just because you have a snowball doesn't mean you have an employee issue. A snowball simply means you have noticed an irregular performance metric, meaning you noticed something that normally isn't there.

What to do:
See why it's happening.

How to do it:

1. Pull Tom aside and say, "Hi Tom, I value you as an employee." (Always start with something genuinely positive. If you don't value Tom, then don't say that.)

2. Point out the snowball, facts only, not opinions, and then ask Tom a question, "Are you aware that you have been late to work the last two Fridays?"

3. Don't answer Tom's question for him. A Lion Leader will ask and patiently wait for a response. The only acceptable answers are YES or NO. Don't buy into any stories.

a. **Tom answers "Yes, I am aware."** Then respond with "Okay, can I ask **WHY** you have been late?" Tom should give a reasonable answer. The fact is that when Tom acknowledges that he is aware, he is taking accountability for his actions and he also knows that he is on your radar.

b. **Tom answers "NO, I am NOT aware."** This is why Lion Leaders only deal with facts. You would then state confidently the facts. "Tom, Last Friday (date) you showed up to work at 9:40 without calling and today you showed at 9:45. Normally you are in the office by 8:55." Then respond with, "Can I ask **WHY** you have been late?" Tom should give a reasonable answer.

4. Next ask Tom for a commitment to get back on track and ask Tom what HE thinks is a reasonable solution for him to get back on track. This approach will usually melt the snowball.

This process allows you to ask questions without accusing, and lets the employee answer and own accountability for their actions. In addition, they feel empowered, not accused, when they can talk through and provide their own P.O.A. (Plan of Action) to resolve their own matter.

The Big RIP in Your Business

Most businesses today are operating without formal infrastructure for: hiring, training, and performance management. There are three critical areas that will determine the success of any organization or could very well tear it apart:

1. **Resources: what you use** (systems, tools, technology, training)
2. **Infrastructure: how you do it** (processes)
3. **People: who does it and measures it** (skill and desire are the two primary reasons why people succeed or fail)

I cannot emphasize enough to hire the right people, who want to do a job and verify that they know how to do it. Then, train them properly on why they are doing it and how to do it better. When you give qualified people the proper resources and support for the right results, you significantly increase both of your chances for success.

Resources –

We are seeing people experience failure today, in some instances, because they simply don't have the right tools to do their job. Notice my use of the word 'right.' Ensure that all of your employees in each role have everything that they need as a resource in order to be successful. Don't assume that they have what they need.

Stay engaged and ask each person specific questions at monthly or quarterly intervals. Here is an example:

What do you need from me or the organization to generate results above the highest standards?

Then close your mouth, open your ears and take notes, take action, and follow up to ensure that resource was what they did indeed need. This way if someone down the road says "I'm failing because I didn't have _____ as a resource," you can address the snowball with facts, not emotions, and bring balance.

Infrastructure –
Your processes should be aligned with the skill level of the person doing the work. Staff needs to be trained on why they are doing a job, not just how to do it.

- **Do they truly understand the purpose of the work?**
- **Do they know who it is benefitting and why?**

Processes should be easy to understand and transferrable to any new staff. This keeps your business adaptable, scalable, and relevant. Today, we see organizations that put people through training that was established many years ago. The staff comes out of training and still doesn't know what to do or why they are doing it. The result is low performance. The company then reacts, gets upset, takes action to penalize the employee with a write-up, and then fires them. It's cyclical.

Regarding the RIP, years ago the difficult thing was consulting with businesses who did not believe they needed a website. At the same time, most were complaining because they were losing business. However, since they lacked infrastructure for measurement of growth, they couldn't tell me how or why they were losing business. When this happens, companies resort to blame: it's a bad market or I can't find good employees. Back then, when I pointed out that a website is not an expense, but a tool to grow new clients and measure traffic, buyers, and losses, their minds changed.

Today, business owners need to take a similar approach with the changing market, social media and technology. People look for careers, shop, buy, learn, and make decisions differently. With the onset and advances in technology, change will continue to happen at a rapid pace. Business owners must keep up. A Lion Leader builds people, provides resources, and challenges the existing infrastructure with purpose, profitability, and vision.

People -
Regardless of how well you build your infrastructure and develop your processes, the foundation of any business starts with building your people. Everyone must know why they are doing what they are doing and they must believe in the company vision. Most leadership today does not establish, know, or even buy into their own vision. This is

extremely important because it lays the framework for the categories above. If you don't have purpose, a mission, and a vison for your organization, how can you expect your new hires and employees to know what to believe in or to follow? Without vision, employees become task-oriented and default to just doing a "job." You want your new hires and other employees working for something bigger than that, otherwise you will start to see attrition. People don't just want a job, they want purpose. Things change when employees work for more than just a paycheck. Understand their need and communicate why you are hiring and what you need. Make sure the role is a fit for both of you. This starts at the hiring process.

Three Factors for People Success

Managing tasks is difficult enough, managing people can be like cat wrangling. Instead, choose to be a leader of people and operate with a solid plan. A plan makes it easier on you and on them. In dealing with many types of people over the last few decades, I have concluded that there are only three key factors that affect, impact, and will determine whether or not an individual will be successful. Earlier we talked about the big RIP in business; this has to do with three factors that impact your organization. This section deals specifically with **people** and the three reasons why they fail or succeed:

1. **Skill –**

   An individual should always be developing the skill-set relative to the line of work and specialty that they are committed to for a living. As a Lion Leader, your job is to ensure, during the interview process, that you are aligning the skill-set of the person directly with the needs of the organization. If you hire an unskilled tradesman for a job that requires mastery, you will get what you hired, and it is your own fault, not theirs. When an individual lacks skill, it is because you under-hired or you placed them in the wrong role. Either way, they will eventually fail as they struggle to meet the demands of the role they are unqualified for. Likewise, a highly skilled employee hired into a mastery role will succeed, assuming these next two components are in place.

2. **Resources –**

   If a person knows how to do a job, you must also provide the right tools to do the job. This seems simple enough, but resources are often neglected as we go about our daily business routines. The risk with not providing the right resources to your professional staff is that they will not perform properly, or at a level that they need to. As a result, their morale will suffer. During one-on-ones, match results back to performance, and back track to look for any deficiencies. Seek to understand why. You can usually isolate the cause back to a resource issue if the skill level is in line. For your sales staff, this can mean having the right CRM, phone system, features, mobile technology, support resources, or even other departments.

3. **Desire** –

My research has shown that when an employee has the right skill-set (trained or hired in with it) and when they are provided with the right resources (relative to the results needed), then logically the only other factor that will affect their success is their desire, either to do the job at all, at a mediocre level, or exceptionally. This is a tricky one, because although you can provide training and tools, you cannot give someone desire. As a leader, this is why snowballs are so important. When you are paying attention to your team, you can quickly identify deficiencies and take the appropriate action to resolve them in any of these three areas. Understand that you must be engaged, because you can misdiagnose. For example, an employee who is working in a role with a low skill-set or without the right resources might have a morale issue that can be categorized incorrectly as a lack of desire.

When it comes to desire, your goal as a leader is to understand:
-   **WHAT** is happening (the behavior)
-   To figure out **WHY** it is happening (the cause)
-   The plan of action **HOW** to fix it (the solution)

Team cultures are unique because every team and every organization is different. However, there is one constant: you are working with people. A Lion Leader understands this and is committed to investing time in hiring the right people and to building those people over time. A culture is only as good as what the leader lets it become. Cultures decline as people learn what is expected, but do what is accepted. When a team learns that gossip, lack of accountability, complacency, and mediocre performance are not addressed,
they will accept these negative attributes as standards. The end result is a dysfunctional culture in decline.

To become a great organization, you must challenge your team to recognize their greatness. Bring disruptive change to your team or organization by setting new standards. Raise the bar and encourage or praise when people over-perform. Then, evaluate performance to continue to attain the desired results. Train and/or discipline immediately when you spot unacceptable behavior that can compromise the health of your team. Recognize and watch for snowballs. Lion Leaders are perceptive and engaged. They help their people uncover what they didn't even know they had inside. They expect and praise performance and never tolerate mediocrity. When your team sees that everyone is in this together, you go from just being a team, to creating a bond, just like a pride of lions. A team works together, a pride trusts each other and holds each other accountable; that is the true key to growing your culture.

**"Motivating people who lack
skill, resources, or desire
creates frustration, not change."**

What type of culture are you building?

Chapter II – Understanding Team Culture

**"A truly strong person does not need
the approval of others any more than
a lion needs the approval of sheep."**
Vernon Howard

Leadership Strategy

I often start off my leadership seminars by asking the attendees to raise their hand if they know the difference between strategy and tactics. This question often prompts wide eyes that roam the room and I rarely see hands raised. The ones that are raised, seem unsure and lack confidence. Besides the fact that this is a poor leadership response, I am amazed that so few people understand these critical leadership tools. My goal is not to bore you with academic details, so I'll explain to you as I do in my seminars:

Strategy is what happens from the neck up. It involves using the brain to formulate the plans to take action. Strategy is the thought behind the action. I say that leaders who over-strategize have big heads, not ego-wise, but full of thought. You could say that they 'think' too much. This is a character trait typically found in the Detailed Leadership Style outlined in Chapter I.

Tactics, on the other hand, are what happen below the neck. Although you can use a 'verbal' tactic, the point to remember is that a tactic requires action. I refer to leaders who use heavy tactics without strategy, as having big feet. Of course, if you have big feet and you are walking around without a plan, you are going to do some significant damage. That is precisely what happens when we use tactics without proper strategies: we become ineffective, create more damage, and our results suffer.

Strategy is an art for planning to execute. It requires time and thought to troubleshoot, mitigate risks, and align with the best possible outcomes. In this chapter, I am going to outline several strategies that you can start using today to impact your new Lion Leadership style. Eventually, your goal should be to positively influence the culture and results of your organization.

Level-Setting (Staying in balance)
As I mentioned earlier, most organizations operate ineffectively because they are out of balance. Being out of balance simply means that your resources, infrastructure, or people are not aligned for optimal results. With resources, it could be that you have a team member who is not trained properly or who doesn't have the right tools to effectively

do their job. Since we know that most people don't speak up about issues to seek resolution, we can conclude that those people are not operating effectively. Therefore, we can say they are out of balance.

As a leader, if any individual facet of your organization is out of balance, you must take immediate action to Level-Set and get back in balance. Being out of balance refers to a sense of control over the situation. For example, if a client constantly makes demands for free products and services, then you are out of balance and they are in control. They are making requests and you keep giving. The goal is not for you to fight for control, because then you would be out of balance again, but to gain a happy medium. Being in balance means that you are Level-Set.

LEVEL SET
Stay in Balance

Culture
Clients
Results
Processes
Relationships

© 2016 MikeRodriguezInternational.com

We frequently see that being out of balance can also apply to employees dealing with other employees or it can happen between an employee and a leader.

I recently worked with a client who had an employee who constantly challenged the leader in just about every forum. The employee would interrupt meetings with negative and unnecessary comments and they would frequently show up late to work. The interesting thing was that the employee produced an excellent quality of work. The leader pointed out that they knew the behavior wasn't right, but they just weren't sure how to fix it. By the way, this example is a common occurrence in the workplace with reckless competitors. The reason the leader felt something was wrong was because they were out of balance with the employee. They weren't Level-Set.

You have to learn to trust your instincts. When you don't take immediate and decisive action to Level-Set a situation like this, the situation will only get worse and you will lose your leverage over time. You will eventually see your team culture start to suffer as they watch your lack of leadership give in to the poor behavior that you are accepting. You are teaching your team to be unbalanced and how to treat you. As a side note, never allow disrespect or a challenge in your office, in your meeting, or in a group setting from anyone. This is a great way to lose your Level-Set and damage your culture.

If a person does say something to disrupt, just say their name followed by "You and I can discuss that in my office after the meeting." Then don't skip a beat and just go back to what you were saying.

If they speak up in an inappropriate way again, say their name again followed by "Please go ahead and excuse yourself from the meeting. I'll meet you in my office afterwards." This shows that you mean business, that you don't accept the behavior, and that you are in control. You have Level-Set the situation they disrupted.

How to Level-Set when you are out of balance:

1. **Recognize the imbalance** and identify if you have lost control or if you have too much control.
2. **Identify WHAT** is happening or what has happened to create the unbalanced situation (facts here, not opinions).
3. **Learn WHY** it is happening (the cause).
4. **Take ACTION** to resolve the WHY and to address the WHAT to get back in balance.

Understand that every challenging or difficult situation you are in didn't happen overnight. Therefore, it will require a certain amount of time, action, and skill to resolve and level most situations.

When you don't take immediate and decisive action to Level-Set, the situation will only get worse and you will lose your leverage over time.

Questions as a Strategy (QaaS)

Regardless of the situation you are in with your team, an employee, or a client, you can effectively work through it if you manage yourself and the situation properly. This takes work and practice with your communication skills. The secret strategy to improving the way you get results and stay in balance, is your ability to shift from making statements, to asking questions. I call it Questions as a Strategy.

When an employee hears a statement from you, whether it is, "Your performance is unacceptable" or "You need to get better results," from their perspective, all they hear is YOU voicing your opinion and attacking them. The impact is minimal. Most of us know this and that is why we have resorted to elevating our voices or sometimes even yelling when we need to address an important matter, or worse, we just email them. A Lion Leader recognizes this strategy, knows they have authority, and communicates effectively by turning statements INTO questions.

Example:
Ineffective way: "Your performance is unacceptable."
QaaS: "Is your current performance in-line with your true potential?" (Then be quiet, listen, and wait.)

Ineffective way: "We need to get better results."
QaaS: "Are we getting the best possible results from you?"

In either of these situations, you have put the accountability for the matter back on the person, prompting them to answer the question with their own words. When they answer the question with the word NO in their own voice, there is power in accountability and ownership of their deficiency. It is much more effective than you pointing it out to them. This gives you leverage and the opportunity to ask yet another question to their own answer.

There is greater power in resolving a matter when an employee acknowledges it rather than you telling them about it.

By asking questions instead of resisting the urge to make statements, you are actually empowering the person to recognize the problem. In my interactions with other leaders and team members using this strategy, both say they felt appreciated and respected. In addition, you are giving them a chance to see that the issue is their responsibility to own and correct, not yours. Finally, the ultimate result is to let them know that you are addressing the behavior at hand, not that you are taking action against them. Any situation that requires two people interacting should always follow the strategy of using QaaS as often as possible. With this strategy, you can isolate the issue, find common ground, and you can start moving towards resolving the matter at hand. As with any life skill, you must practice this. You will have a natural tendency to fall back into your old routines and make statements. However, as you practice, you will recognize opportunities to rephrase your statements into questions for maximum effectiveness. This especially comes in handy when you are dealing with challenging situations or work related problems with employees. Just be sure that your questions don't come off as an interrogation or as being manipulative.

Correcting Poor Behavior

When you get to a point where you can improve your communication to a mastery level of asking questions vs. making statements, your team will start to see it and you will feel it. Others will perceive this approach as you taking a vested interest in who they are. The results will be extremely positive and well received. Occasionally though, we all encounter issues with employees who exhibit poor behavior:

- **An employee who is not doing what they need to do, or**
- **An employee who is doing something they shouldn't be doing.**

Learn to recognize these two scenarios as behavioral related. The point that you should take away from this section is that a Lion Leader will always separate the behavior from the person:

- WHO they are

  vs.

- WHAT they are or are not doing

Lion Leaders always separate
the behavior from the person

Separating the behavior from the person, means that you recognize that each person has value, skill, and their own actions. Your job is to help them to feel value and continually develop their skills, while you help them to address the results or consequences of their actions, or lack thereof. In other words, we always love the employee, but we might not like or approve of what **they are doing or not doing**.

Employee behavior should be separated into two categories:

1. **Business Impacting** - Business impacting matters include, but are not limited to, any actions or behaviors that will have an immediate, direct, or long term NEGATIVE impact on any person, process, or resource within or affiliated with the organization. This includes client interaction. Examples might include any action that violates a law or that compromises your company code of conduct or ethics standards.

2. **NON-Business Impacting** - These matters are important and should be addressed, but shouldn't be blown out of proportion. Snowballs (at different levels) usually fall into this category. These typically involve

more day-to-day issues that need to be contained before they grow into business impacting matters. This includes but is not limited to things like: attitudes, tardiness, low performance, and personnel and client situations.

The reason we identify and separate behaviors that are business impacting is because we want to stay in balance. You don't want to stress out over every matter that comes up within a day.

You must learn to:
- **Identify** the situation first
    o **What** is happening.
    o **Why** it is happening.

- **Make a decision** on how and when you are going to address the behavior with the employee. After you identify any matter and you categorize it, then you must take the appropriate action to put together a plan to resolve it immediately.

Live Talks vs. Digital
Technology was meant to make our lives easier, not to replace our ability to be more effective. If you have a personnel issue, there is not a better way to miscommunicate and dilute your message than by sending an email, text, or instant message.

In its basic form, it is cowardice to avoid a live talk. Consider it irresponsible and lazy. In more complicated matters, it can be considered negligence. Don't take the easy way out and don't be lazy. Your best impact, is to always talk in person or to pick up the phone.

Managing Employee Performance

I rarely meet leaders who like to deal with problem employees, problem areas, or who like to take disciplinary action. Yes, it is uncomfortable and that is precisely why you should take action. Delayed or overlooked attention to unacceptable performance is a leading cause of broken cultures and declines in revenue growth. The risks of not dealing with a business impacting matter now will be much greater and create more liability later on. In addition, you are actually contributing to the demise of your culture when you avoid important matters. You also expose your organization to more risk.

Here is why:

Contrary to what you believe, most people within your organization and almost all of your peer or subordinate leaders are aware of issues with personnel. They are also very aware of what you do and what you do not do. Your actions as a leader set the precedent and tempo for everyone else to follow. When you overlook poor performance, the team sees this as acceptance. You are teaching them how to build your culture and who you are as a leader. This is why the Lion Leadership style is so critical. Lion Leaders understand that the overall health of the team is determined by their ability to stay engaged, focused, and remain in line with the vision.

When it comes to employee performance, the key here is to:

- **Clarify** why you are talking to the person. I always ask: "Do you know why we are meeting?" If they say YES, I have THEM explain why. It brings more accountability and balance to our conversation when they say it. If they say NO, then I:

- **Identify the issue** – Be specific using only facts not emotions about the matter. Remember to separate the behavior from the person. Also, turn your statements into questions. As an example, you wouldn't say "You're not doing a very good job, so I am going to write you up." You would ask:
  - o **YOU: Do you know why we are meeting?**
  - o **Them: Yes, it's because I am missing my targets.**
  - o **YOU: Yes that is correct.**

Next you would outline:
1. **WHAT is happening**
2. **WHY it's happening**
3. **HOW the two of you will work together to correct it**

- **Catch it early** – Review the section on Snowballs. Small things are always easier to resolve than larger ones. In addition, the employee will also feel that they have a chance to succeed, because they know they are valued as they own the performance issue.

- **Only talk facts** – People can't argue with data. Let them know exactly what the issue is with examples and details. Recall the dates and times and targets, if necessary, that you have established.

- **Put together a P.O.A. (Plan of Action) with metrics** – If you don't know what you need them to accomplish and if you or they cannot measure the results, you won't see progress. Be specific with dates and times and what type(s) of specific and measurable action you need to see. Don't say "I need you to improve," instead say, "We need your current performance of 75% increased to 85% by the end of the month, and then to 100% by the next quarter.

- **Follow up (accountability)** – Ensure that the standards are being met and kept. Set and keep follow up meetings with them. Review missed areas/metrics, talk about and encourage improvements and commend them only when they have exceeded the expectations.

When you talk with some employees about their performance, you will find that they like to deflect the attention from themselves to something else or to someone else. This is called an emotional distraction, because they defend their claim with emotions; they might get angry, cry, or take on some kind of emotional state to gain empathy and to draw attention away from them and back to you or their claim. They are hoping that you buy their defense.

A Lion Leader is conscientious of people and their feelings, but is smart enough to know that when you have real facts and true data, people can't effectively deflect. It's hard to argue with data.

As a Lion Leader, your goal is not to argue, but instead, to:

- **Not get drawn into the drama,**
- **Stay with the facts, and**
- **Head towards resolution to correct the performance.**

You do this by asking them questions, based on facts, that they can agree to. Find common ground together. You can only head towards resolution once you can help them to:

- **Recognize** both of your positions
- **Understand** the situation
- **Acknowledge** the deficiency
- **Accept** the facts and own it

76

For clarification purposes, a Lion Leader will never use data as leverage to manipulate. We only use it to:

- **Validate a deficiency or performance issue**
- **Gain agreement and understanding**

This is done for the health and progress of the person and the team.

Facts vs. Opinions

Opinions are what you (or they) think. Facts are what is actually going on. Make your decisions based on facts, not on your emotions. There is a time for sympathy and for empathy, but don't be tempted to fall back on empathy all of the time; you will lose your leverage as a leader. It doesn't require a forensics expert to validate that business cultures today have become out of balance. This has developed as a result of our inattention to poor behavior and our lack of attention to adequately address it. One of the core causes of this challenge in the workplace, and in our society in general, is that we have completely confused and accepted opinions over facts, as the truth. With the continued growth of technology and social media, we are seeing more and more individuals who are sharing their thoughts and emotions with the general public on a larger and larger scale. As logical professionals, we have slowly been indoctrinated to believe what we read and what we hear is truth. When we read the written thoughts and opinions of emotionally driven and passionate people, some feel they have no other choice but to be drawn into the situation. As a result, we sometimes wrongfully accept one person's opinion as fact, or truth.

In our world today, we let opinions affect politics, relationships, religion, and the way we buy, talk, eat, and sleep. Opinions also have a big impact in the workplace. I recently was working with a client who had this type of opinion-driven employee. Whenever the employee was confronted about their poor performance, the employee would deflect the matter back to the leader and validate that the problem was with the leader or with something else. For example, in one situation when the employee was confronted about their poor performance, the employee told the leader, "I feel like you don't like me and that you are out to get me" (deflection, back to the leader). Most leaders today would respond to this with empathy and take ownership of the claim, validating it in the mind of the employee. However, a quick analysis of this statement reveals that it is driven by emotion and contains no facts or data, only the emotional driven opinion of the employee.

In this situation, the leader, wanting to appease the employee, was too soft and apologized to the employee for the employees claim. The risk with this situation now, is that the employee believed that their opinion of the boss not liking them is real (although it in fact, isn't) and that the boss is indeed out to get the employee (false too). In addition, the true matter (the performance) had been completely overlooked. All of this drama was created by the passion-driven opinions of the employee and an improperly trained leader who reacted to the opinion. A Lion Leader isn't influenced by opinions or manipulated by emotion. A Lion Leader only deals with facts, that's all. Lion Leaders know that opinions are driven by emotions, that emotions are messy and they usually favor the control of the employee. This creates an imbalance. Our goal is not to gain control, but to stay in balance for the benefit of everyone. Lion Leaders always handle themselves with calm confidence and act from a position of strength.

Here is a proper Lion Leadership response to "I feel like you don't like me and that you are out to get me:"
LL - Repeat: "If I am hearing you correctly, you are saying that you feel like I don't like you and that I am out to get you, is that correct?" – This allows the employee to rethink their claim and confirms that you are listening.
Employee: Yes or No – If they say NO, ask them to restate what they said. If they say YES:
LL - Address the Claim/Deflection Directly: Let me assure you that I do indeed like you, and that I am not out to get you.
LL - Highlight the Behavior: However, I am not happy with and I do not like your performance.
LL - Get Back in Balance: Do you understand that as a leader I have the right and responsibility to address performance matters with employees?

Employee: Yes or No – If they say NO, ask them why they believe that. If they say YES, you are back in balance.

Remember that any employee corrective action should be taken seriously and communicated in such a way that there is no misinformation. If necessary, have a co-leader or HR representative in the meeting with you.

Strategies to know about Disciplinary Action or Termination:
- Conduct these meetings in a formal setting (office or conference room), no coffee shops or public places.
- Bring your documentation. (so make sure you are documenting).
- Be prepared with your facts, dates and details.
- Treat everyone fairly and with respect. What you do for one person, you must do for all.
- These ARE NOT NEGOTIATIONS. Don't get sidetracked. Deliver your message, outline the next steps, then allow them to leave and get back to work.
- Always consult with HR or corporate counsel when in doubt.

Always end with encouragement. When people believe that you have their best interest at heart and that you have faith in their ability to recover, they will surprise you by the actions they will take.

Micro-Managing vs. Accountability
We have many major challenges with people as the world continues to change. This is another great reason why each of us needs to adopt a Lion Leadership mindset and philosophy. One of the great challenges with teams today is that we have lost sight of accountability. Leaders have become soft, as not to offend, and as a result, people have confused accountability with micro-managing. I see this on a daily basis, leaders who fear holding people accountable because they don't want to be perceived as micro-managers. I also see employees who defend their lack of accountability by falsely claiming as the self-proclaimed company spokesman, "We are being micro-managed." It's a chronic problem that needs to be corrected today.

For the sake of understanding, let me clarify the definition of both of these terms so we understand what is really going on:
Micro-Managing is having control of every part of a person or activity, no matter how small.

Accountability is the fact or condition of being accountable and responsible for yourself, another, or an activity.

> **Micro-managing is excessive involvement.**
> **Accountability is ensuring someone is being**
> **responsible for what they are supposed to do.**
> **This is also called effective leadership.**

What I have found is that when an employee or a person claims that they or others are being micro-managed, they are almost always deflecting from their lack of wanting to be accountable. It's easier to call you a micro-manager than it is to say 'I'm not doing my job' or 'I don't want to be held accountable.' A Lion Leader identifies three things to offset this mindset and to neutralize and eliminate these claims:

1. **That each employee hired is empowered to do their job and expected to attain the results that they were hired in to do.**
2. **If they aren't attaining the results, that the deficiency must be addressed with facts, not emotions.**
3. **If an employee claims micro-managing, a Lion Leader simply asks the employee to give an example of how they are being micro-managed.**

Once again, the Lion Leader is looking for facts, not opinions. If the employee produces facts, the Lion Leader acknowledges the facts and puts together a plan with the employee to get back in balance. If the employee produces their opinion, then the Lion Leader shares facts with questions and seeks agreement to their action to get back in balance.

If you lead by caring what people think about you, you will always be limited by their opinions.

Your Best One-on-One

All of the strategies I have covered so far can and should be used during your one-on-ones. If you are not consistently having one-on-ones with team members every week, you are cheating yourself and your team. A one-on-one is an employee's meeting to share information with you. It is a dedicated time for just the two of you, set at a specific time each week, usually up to 30 minutes, to be used as a check-in and a check-up with each team member. Should be in person, or video for remote employees.

A Question for you: If you could catch and correct a problem area with a team member, when would you want to catch it? Sooner or later? An effective one-on-one allows you to catch it sooner. When you consider that employees can move quickly from one stage to another, Competitor to Complacent and so on, you understand that you have a responsibility to stay involved to catch and correct behaviors.

Risks to one-on-ones:
- **Don't make the content routine.**
- **Make sure you are mentally and physically present. Both of these are important because the one-on-one will lose its value quickly if you aren't engaged and the meeting isn't beneficial to both of you.**
- **Don't let the one-on-one lose its importance.**

NEVER use a one-on-one as a forum to discipline an employee. The one-on-one should be considered their time to check in, share success, and update matters with you that they need help with or that you have noticed. Yes, you can point out snowballs, but never reprimand an employee or put an employee on a disciplinary plan during their one-on-one. Schedule separate meetings and/or times for that.

Content and Delivery:
The content should be question driven: YOU asking questions, listening, and them responding with answers or solutions. The delivery should be positive and engaging. Avoid generalizations and closed ended questions. Don't say: How are things going? Or: Are you having a great week? Instead ask questions that require communication, answers, and feedback. Some leaders have great content when communicating, but they fail in their delivery with either their voice inflection, message tone or expression. Others have great delivery, but lack in content of what they are saying, why they are saying it and what they mean. Content and delivery are both critical tools of communication for any leader in any situation, but they are great practice points during a one-on-one.

Your one-on-one should have a consistent flow, without being too routine, and should always have a takeaway or action item for the employee.

Flow example:
- **Greet and ask first open ended question**
- **Recap key points from the last one-on-one**
  - ○ **Ask for updates on the last action items**
    - ▪ **Be specific and get specific answers**
- **Ask "What are your top two challenging areas this week?"**
  - ○ **Don't accept 'none' as an answer**
- **Ask "What do you need from me to address them?"**
- **Listen and take notes**
- **Ask "What else do you need from me?"**
- **Share what you have noticed this week about them.**
  - ○ **Positives and areas of improvement**
  - ○ **Remember this is not a disciplinary meeting**
- **Establish new action items**
- **Gain agreement on them**
- **End**

For the Competitors - It is permissible to have one-on-ones every other week, but you must still meet to simply stay visible, and keep them on track. You can keep these meetings short to under five minutes.

For Complacent employees - You need to hold one-on-one meetings once a week. For those of you who say that is too much and too soon, that is only your emotions talking.

Remember, if you aren't staying engaged with your team, you will start to have issues, slowly but surely.

For Complainers - If they are already on a performance plan, I recommend that you meet at least once a day. This should also apply to any employee who is not performing or who has a deficiency. If they're not on a performance plan, this doesn't have to be a formal meeting, just a check-in. This will allow you the opportunity to stay involved and provide the assistance that they need.

Everything is Awesome!
Are you giving too much praise? I once heard that you cannot give too much praise; this is simply not true. Part of the breakdown in the business world today is that we have a segment of people constantly seeking praise for work that they are supposed to be doing! When you give too much praise, you establish a sense of false accomplishment. This perpetuates the narcissistic employee mindset and actually limits performance. Why should someone over-perform if they are getting praise and rewards for just doing their job?

Lion Leaders never give praise for menial tasks or standard tasks that people are simply required to do. A warm "thank you" is sufficient. Today, if someone just does a job, we see some leaders who throw around praise saying things like "great job" for every employee and for jobs that weren't great, they were just completed.

If you are having a hard time understanding this, you could be too emotionally attached to your behavior.

It is okay and proper to thank someone for completing a task, or to genuinely let them know that you appreciate that they do their work on time. However, if someone simply does their job, they have done their job. That is what they are paid to do. Again, don't over reward basic or standard behavior. It throws your culture out of balance and actually lowers performance standards by creating a false sense of accomplishment. Instead, challenge your team and encourage them to be more and do more, THEN you can lay on praise heavy so everyone can see it and feel it. This strategy drives a new behavior and causes others to set a new standard.

Chapter III – Leadership Strategy

Are you promoting a culture of growth and change or have you become complacent?

Chapter III – Leadership Strategy

**"Direction starts with a belief system.
What people believe in
is what they will follow."**
Mike Rodriguez

IV

Establishing the Vision

The core of attaining success as a leader falls back on your dedication to your cause and the discipline to take action with purpose and precision. It can be difficult to identify and act on what you need to do vs. what you want to do. The reason is that these types of decisions are heavily influenced by emotions, which can override the foundation of your belief system.

Around 480 BC, a very small group of Greek soldiers, led by King Leonidas of Sparta, fought and encountered major success during one of the most highlighted battles of that time. Although the Spartans finally fell to the Persian army after about seven days, they created a story that will always be remembered. Even though he won, I'm sure Xerxes, the leader of the Persians was disappointed, confused, and overwhelmed by the final results. Xerxes Persian armies of about 150,000 soldiers greatly outnumbered the 7,000 Greek Spartans. Eventually the Spartan army was reduced to only 300, yet they still kept going strong.

Why? What was the difference?

Leonidas was a Lion Leader who had deeply shared the vision with his Spartan soldiers. They believed it, accepted it, and lived it. Not only that, but they believed in and loved their leader. They were fighting for more than a war; they were fighting together for their cause. Xerxes armies, on the other hand, were fighting because they were told to. Although they eventually won, it was not from determination, but from having a much greater number of soldiers. Still, the undeniable purpose and vision of the Spartans caused massive damage to the Persians, even though they were significantly outnumbered. The Spartans were competitors and they were fighting to win. They had a vision that was bigger than them, so they fought to defy the odds. The Persians, on the other hand, were complacent or reckless competitors, doing what they were supposed to do.

The end result is that today we talk about the amazing accomplishments of the Spartan 300, even though they lost to the larger Persian army.

Job vs. Results

My intent isn't to compare the workplace to a battle. My goal is to reinforce with you as a leader, that if your team is results oriented vs. tasked oriented, and working with and towards a vison, the results can be unbelievable. The most successful teams and organizations have evolved to work for something bigger. They are working towards their own vision. When people understand these things, then they can create a results oriented environment:

- WHY they are doing a job,
- WHAT the benefit is to them and everyone else
- HOW to do the job properly with purpose
- THAT they have a leader worthy of following

**Managers create routines and policy,
Leaders create vision-based results.**

Previously in my career, I received multiple awards at an organization for having the top performing team for multiple months & quarters. At the end of one year, I received the top leadership award as a result of the overall performance of my team for the year. Shortly thereafter, I was approached by someone who asked me, "How is it that your team is always number one and how do you hire great people?" I told him that I didn't hire great people, I hired regular people who wanted to become great. I let him know that I worked with them, shared the team vision, and eventually they chose to become part of it. They owned it and as a result, they were working each day for the vison and not for a job.

How did we stay number one? That was easy, everyone on my team expected us to be number one. When we hired someone new, they realized very quickly what they were a part of and that they had to make a decision to step up their game. They took ownership to be part of our 'pride' of performance-based loyalty. We worked together towards something bigger than us: our vison.

- **Is your team task oriented or results oriented?**
- **Do you manage tasks or do you lead to results?**
- **Does your team see the vision or do they have a job?**

Employee Engagement – Align with the Vision

When you considered the data I shared earlier about the high percentage of complacent employees, it is very apparent that we have a lack of engagement issue. With almost seven out of ten employees just going through the motions, it is time for us to recognize that we have a major problem. This problem can be fixed, but we must be willing to accept it as a problem first and then we need leaders who are willing to step up and take the right action.

During leadership trainings, I often show a picture of a farmer herding sheep. When you turn the page, take a closer look and make note of what you see.

If you actually take time to look at the photo, you will see that the man in the picture is managing, not leading. The sheep are only doing as they are told or directed to do. They are not focused, and their eyes are the true giveaway. Ironically, the man feels in control. There is no vision. This is an example of a task oriented work environment with an ineffective, authoritative manager and people who are just going through the motions doing as they are told.

- Is the man in the picture managing or leading?
- What about the sheep?
- What stands out about them?
- Do they look focused?
- Look at their eyes, what do you see?
- What stands out about the picture?

Now consider this next picture. Take a closer look and make note of what you see.

- **Is this group being managed or being led?**
- **What about the entire pride?**
- **What stands out about them?**
- **Do they look focused?**
- **Look at their eyes, what do you see?**

All eyes are forward. Every team member is involved, engaged, and committed to the vision, each in their own way. Some are falling behind, some are in the middle, and some are in front. As a third party viewer, it is very difficult to know who the leader of the pride is, because the leader doesn't have to display dominance. The leader knows who they are and they are there to keep the team in balance. The team knows where they are going and the direction of their eyes is validation. They all can see it, with their minds and then with their eyes.

There is a very strong contrast between these two images. The lion pride is a testament to an engaged team who is following a purpose bigger than each individual team member. However, they have come to terms to understand and accept that they are indeed important. They believe that they are a valuable part of the team.

**When people can see what YOU see
and believe in it and you,
they will follow.**

Your Mission Statement
If you need people to follow you, you better know who you are. It seems easy enough to say that all organizations should have a written mission statement, but many don't. I also find that the mission statements that do exist were put together like marketing campaigns: all for show.

A mission statement should define and outline the purpose that will get you to the vision. It will come only after much thought and input from team members who are truly committed to the cause. Any mission statement written with the purpose of just having a mission statement is about as effective as reading the ingredients on a bottle of shampoo. It is just a bunch of meaningless words. I dare you to reevaluate your mission statement and to ensure that it is a true statement that represents the mission you are committed to accomplish. If you haven't written one, start today. Get your most trusted advisors and leaders together in a room and talk live. Challenge each other and promote thought. Don't accept clichés.

Once you can gain agreement on your mission statement, write it down, and then commit it in writing. Have it printed on a large sign for everyone to see when they visit your office(s). If you feel uncomfortable with this suggestion, then you are already compromising yourself as a Lion Leader. You should be proud of your team, your organization, and where you plan to go. Start requiring that people get educated on your mission statement during new hire on-boarding. Have a meeting to ensure your staff knows it and that they understand the importance and commitment behind it.

15 Qualities of a Lion Leader

We have established that there are three types of people, and we have identified leadership styles. Which type are you? Be honest. Figure out which level you are at, why you are there, and then decide if you are willing to move up. Early in my career I was a machine, a reckless competitor! I pushed people. We closed a lot of business, lost a lot of business, and had no referrals. Most managers are like this, because they are focused on the wrong objective: to satisfy their own needs. When we talk about "Lion Leaders," we understand that they have developed certain defining qualities. The important thing is that they know who they are. They accept the responsibility of their role and they act in a way that is consistent with how they see themselves as leaders. When you know who you are, you'll know who you are not, and you can acknowledge or strengthen your defining qualities. Every Lion Leader that I have trained has made a decision to acquire these 15 qualities, without negotiation. For some it is a work in progress and for others they are working on moving from memorizing to internalizing. Their goal is to master them.

1. Trust – They have established trust through their actions. They also believe in the team and give trust to others, so they will become trustworthy.
2. Balance – Lion Leaders stay aligned with their team, their clients and the organization.
3. Confidence – They realize that people follow and believe in those that believe in who they are.
4. Focus – They keep their minds on the results and avoid temporary distractions. Regardless of the outcome, they see what others can't see.
5. Purpose Driven – They know that without beliefs, action won't happen. Lion Leaders create personal accountability that inevitably transfers to their team.
6. Willingness to Keep Learning – They agree that they never know it all, so they continually learn and apply the knowledge.
7. Doers, Not Talkers – They consistently take action. They fail often to keep succeeding!

8. Positive Attitude – They know that their attitude is contagious and establishes the tempo for them and for others.
9. Encouragers – They help people to recognize their potential even when they cannot see it.
10. Listeners - Lion Leaders learn to stop and really listen. They are genuine, focused, and convey purpose in communication.
11. Results Oriented Persistence – They deliver results, not excuses. They work through failure and look for ways to attain or exceed the end result.
12. Patience – They know that great things take time and work. They manage their emotions because they understand that emotions fuel impatience.
13. Courage with Humbled Strength – Lion Leaders aren't afraid to say what needs to be said, not what is popular. They speak up and take action when they need to, knowing that hurt feelings are always better that hurt progress.
14. Discipline – They do what they need to do, when it's time to do it. They recognize that disorganization and procrastination are not leadership qualities.
15. Integrity – they do what is right, when others disagree and even when they stand alone.

When you modify your mindset and behavior, your team will recognize this and will be more willing to commit to the vision with you. Lion Leaders focus on using a system of purpose-based actions: they stop "telling" and start asking questions to ensure that everyone sees the vision. This allows the team to execute effectively and perform above all of the established standards. These qualities can be learned, but they all start with your BELIEF SYSTEM; if you don't believe in them, you won't do them. Start by doing these things:

- Train and motivate yourself daily! (It is not your organization's responsibility, it's yours.)
- Be aware of your daily routines and step it up.
- Create a culture of performance - This means no gossip, negative talk, or mediocrity.
- Ask yourself: Is what I'm doing allowing me to exceed my goals? If not, change your actions and mindset, TODAY!
- Stop following the herd! Stop acting like and leading like the competition. BE the Competition!

Leadership is an honorable role. Lion Leaders set the new standards that may not be popular, but they are necessary. Leadership positions must be respected and approached as a role of responsibility. You have a responsibility to identify your strengths and weaknesses and to keep improving yourself. So once again, you are faced with another choice. You can say, "Yeah, I've heard this before and I already know this." My answer to you would be: "Yeah, but do you do it?" and "Do you do it ALL of the time?" It's time to step into your potential.

There is never a reason to brag about your position or your title. A lion doesn't have to tell you it's a Lion.

The True CEO

You may or may not be the CEO of your organization, but you are in fact the CEO of your own life. Leaders who can understand and accept this great responsibility are well on their way to becoming the most effective Lion Leader. Accountability starts with you. What you do and how you lead is what others will follow.

As CEO of your own life, you must own that fact that as an employee, you are not hired to perform a job, you are trusted and paid to get a result. Managers view themselves as higher paid employees with titles who lead tasks; Lion Leaders know that they are a valuable resource entrusted to help a team accomplish amazing results. Change the way you see your employment status and you will change the way you perform. Recognize that as an employee, you have really only entered into a business partnership with your current employer. They are outsourcing your skills and talents, in return for a salary and possibly other pay. They are trusting in your abilities to help them attain their biggest targets. When you look at the work situation this way, you can accept accountability for 100% of your actions, because you are in fact, in control. Your employer only assumes control when you aren't performing. This same rule applies to each of your direct reports as well. As you help your team to realize that they aren't just an employee, but that they are a critical part of the team that is working together to accomplish goals, they can start to embrace their new situation as CEO of their own life.

As CEO of your own life, you are responsible for every aspect of your life and the decisions you make, or don't make. A Lion Leader accepts and believes that they are every role that exists in a traditional organization:

Marketing – How you dress and talk represents your brand to others who come in contact with you. Why not be the best-dressed employee at the organization? Excuses not accepted.

Human Resources – What you say and how you conduct yourself with others is your responsibility. Act in a way that represents you well as CEO. Don't create problems, but be a positive resource for others.

Sales – People are making decisions on a daily basis about whether or not they want to do business with you. Be genuine, likeable, and trustworthy. Even if you don't carry a sales title, you my friend are in sales.

Customer Service – How you handle challenges and work through issues with others, creates an example of your character. Don't gossip, argue, or be rude to people.

Yes, these things are going to be difficult to transition to, but Lion Leaders are ready to take on any challenge that will improve themselves or their team members for the greater cause of the organization. Regardless of the character traits listed above, the truth is that it costs you nothing to be a

Lion Leader, but can cost you everything if don't take action to grow.

What if You Fail?

It is acceptable to take two steps up and one step back, as long as you keep going! Thomas Edison said, "Many of life's failures are people who did not realize how close they were to success when they gave up."

When you choose to pursue anything that you are passionate about, including becoming a Lion Leader, you are destined to face failures. It is simply a part of the process of life and mandatory for your journey to success. You must learn to embrace failure, not as a flaw in your character, but merely as an obstacle that you can and should overcome. Failures are basically a learning experience of what "did not" work as part of your process to change, not that "YOU" do not work. Make sure that you understand the difference. If you choose to stop at your next obstacle, then your journey has finished and things will remain the same for you. If you completely give up, that is only when you have truly failed.

Lion Leaders choose to keep going. You might encounter another failure, but through the sheer act of your persistence, you will eventually succeed. Use your failures as an opportunity to re-evaluate and keep going. A mistake that is encountered or created with good intentions is actually a positive result. This means that you are doing something, and through doing that something, you have just discovered what won't work. This may sound odd to you, but it is true.

"Failure isn't WHO you are, it is a RESULT of what you did or did not do."
MIKE RODRIGUEZ
MikeRodriguezInternational.com

Failure should be a positive opportunity for you to realize change.

Once you can learn to step up your tempo and focus on the results instead of the tasks, you will start learning from your mistakes. As a result, you will start to improve as a leader.

**I have made many mistakes in my life.
They do not define me, they refine me.**

The mistakes I have encountered and learned from have created the Lion Leader that I am and they have led me to success. However, holding on to mistakes of your past is indeed a mistake. As you encounter failure and mistakes in your life, that little voice of despair will want you to hold onto those failures as a reminder of your past. You must let them go. You cannot change your past, but you can accept your past, forgive yourself, and you can write a new future, if you choose to. When you encounter failure, remember that this doesn't mean YOU are a failure. Think of the mistakes of the past as heavy weights. Every time you choose to hold on to those mistakes and failures, you are actually choosing to carry that unnecessary weight. After a period of time, you can see that the burden will be entirely too big for you to carry. In fact, it will start to weigh you down and prevent you from moving forward and reaching your full potential. Also, don't let others give you more unnecessary weight in the form of negative words and opinions. That is merely their negativity that you can refuse to accept.

Where you are in your life right now is only temporary, it's up to you to let it become permanent!

Choose to let go of your mediocre past and choose to start writing a new future for yourself today by becoming a Lion Leader. Think of it this way: by writing a new future, taking action on it, and living it, as time progresses, you are actually creating a new past and better memories for yourself. This will allow you to perform better in your career and in your life as you become a Lion Leader.

I Challenge You

In a lion pride when one member decides that they want to lead, they will challenge the leader. When this happens, the challenger has reached a point in their life and in their mind that they believe they are capable, prepared, and ready to lead. The only obstacle that stands in the way is their ability to defeat the existing leader. Their belief system must be validated, they will decide to pursue the coveted spot, and at some point, they will decide to take action.

I challenge you to evaluate and change your belief system and replace yourself with You as a new leader.

What you believe is what you will follow. Know what you are following, understand why, and ensure you are following the right things. Believe that you are capable. Know that you are ready to move your life and your career to the next level. Lion Leaders refuse to think self-doubting thoughts. They are forward thinkers who are constantly looking to improve, because they believe they can and they know they are worthy.

I challenge you to break your routines of being complacent.
Every person has established life and work routines. Yours might have been holding you back, but not anymore. Commit today to start new routines that will take you closer to your goals. Recognize that just because you have been doing something for a long time that you no longer have an excuse to accept it as being right. Just because you have been getting a good result, doesn't mean it's the best way. Lion Leaders recognize and eliminate complacent actions.

I challenge you to become a competitor and to stay at that level.
You may be at a point in your life or career that you don't want to be. Know that you can change if you desire to. Lion Leaders have been complainers and complacent. They realized that wasn't acceptable to them, so they took action to change. They like to win and needed to win. Not for the sake of beating others, but for the sense of accomplishment and fulfillment that it brings in knowing they did their best.

I challenge you to BE the competition.
This means that you are in competition with no one, but yourself. Lion Leaders refocus every morning and relax every night after reviewing their day. They know that if they are performing at their best level, at the best possible moments, then they don't have to worry about anyone else.

I challenge you to rethink your belief system.
Start believing and accepting that you have authority and accept that you are a great leader. You may not be today, but you will be if you believe it. Lion Leaders think about ways to change how they can improve their lives, the lives of others, and the performance of their organization.

I challenge you to no longer negotiate with mediocrity.
Eliminate this major problem from your life and from your organization. Hire competitors, train them to become better, and ensure that they have everything they need to

win. Develop your complacent team members by helping them to realize their purpose and their potential. Lion Leaders refuse to accept excuses, blame, negativity or mediocrity. They recognize that these are symptoms of complainers. They know that complainers create unhealthy cultures and damage performance. Lion Leaders do not tolerate or accept anything that will compromise the success of the team member or of the team.

I challenge you to take action to become a Lion Leader. Lion Leaders are respected, trusted, and loved. Lion Leaders help their teams to discover their courage and to shed their skins of complacency. They establish a vision and help others to realize and believe without a doubt. They inspire others to pursue excellence as a team with complete and unquestioned accountability. Lion Leaders find a way when no one else can see a way. They rise after everyone else has fallen. Their power and strength is manifested in the way they carry themselves: silent and controlled power, for the betterment of the team, to pursue the vision and exceed the expectations of what they were born to do.

Never forget that leadership is a privilege and an honor that few embrace properly, but not you. Leadership requires courage and is not for the weak. Even the sacred texts remind us "To whom much is given, much is expected." Remember that leadership is a responsibility of authority that you have earned and that you should respect. However, it is not necessary to remind people of your authority or to reduce it in an effort to be accepted. Your leaders trust in you and placed you where they need you to be, based on your qualifications.

When you apply the principles in this book, you will get resistance as your team struggles to find their new vision. After time, after challenges, and after tests of endurance by all members of the team, they will come to trust you and love you and what you represent. This can only happen once your team knows that you have their best interest at heart. Don't be afraid to create disruptive change when necessary. People will emotionally deflect and hide behind the false claims of their dislike for you as a leader or that your new policies are not fair. What they really dislike is the accountability to perform and the expectations to step outside of their mediocrity. Stretch their comfort zones.

Whatever your current role is, know that you now have everything you need to start your journey towards success. You just need to recognize it and own it. As you start using the strategies contained in this book, you can effectively change the outcome of your results, the course of your life and the lives of others. I challenge you and ask you to embrace effective teamwork, proven strategies, and clarity of vision as you start your journey to become a Lion Leader.

I have challenged you. What will you do?

I accept the challenge to become a Lion Leader:

_____

Signed

_____

Date

The Final Challenge

We need to continue to grow bold and fearless
Lion Leaders around the world.
I challenge you to help change the course of business and
the quality of people, one person at a time.
I am counting on you to challenge another person to
become a Lion Leader.
Let someone borrow this book or
invest in a copy for them.

I Accept This Challenge:

_____

Chapter IV – Establishing the Vision

"Now, it's time for you to become a Lion Leader.
Go Forth and Make Your Life Exceptional!"
Mike Rodriguez

Tips from Lion Leaders

Tips from Lion Leaders

Effective Communication
Mike Wylie – Chief Executive Officer
Standing Dog Interactive

A couple of years ago, I had a major cultural problem in my then 8-year-old company. I didn't feel as though most of our employees were motivated to perform at their full potential and my best employees were leaving for other opportunities. We were growing fast and I was very concerned. In hindsight, I see we grew so quickly that we unknowingly lost our identity. In the beginning years, I was involved with almost every employee in the company at some level. As our business expanded, a distance grew between myself and my employees. As more management layers were added, this division became even more pronounced. I felt the culture of the company, or lack thereof, began to erode and I knew I needed to turn us in a positive direction.

I began changing our culture by talking to and more importantly *listening* to my employees to understand what was creating this uninviting culture. After gathering feedback, several themes emerged around communication, management, autonomy and training. Some of it was tough to hear, but the bottom line was that I had become an ineffective leader. I wanted to hear more and keep the dialogue going. I researched and found an application, to help me communicate directly with my 70+ employees allowing me to effectively and efficiently communicate with each of them every week. The premise is that employees take 15 minutes each week to answer questions and the manager takes five minutes to review and respond. The responses to this process were enlightening as it gave a voice to many employees who were not comfortable to tell me face-to-face how they were feeling or the things they saw wrong with the company. The more I responded, the more I received in return. I was able to quickly fix many issues ranging from personnel conflicts to recognizing employees that were being overlooked to employees simply wanting an ice machine.

One of requests that resulted from this process was that the employees wanted more frequent news and updates on the progress of the company. I thought it was obvious to everyone that the company was successful since we were turning down business due to our rapid growth. I didn't realize this lack of specific communication combined with good people leaving the company added to the feeling of perceived instability. Further, the employees wondered how effective their managers could possibly be when they couldn't answer seemingly basic questions about the direction of the company. To make matters worse, I unintentionally micromanaged the managers. If there was an issue, they always had to run it by my president or me.

This was enlightening to me as I would never have defined myself as a micromanager yet once I heard the feedback and took I step back, I realized that I was doing just that.

Our managers were not empowered to make decisions whether for a client or employee resulting in an ineffective management structure.

This is when I got to know Mike Rodriguez. My wife attended a conference where he spoke and she encouraged me to reach out to him since he was based in Dallas. He quickly became a great mentor and friend to me. I needed leadership training and his guidance, feedback and encouragement were invaluable to me especially during such a critical turning point in my business. He taught me some much needed leadership skills which I then had him train to my managers and the future leaders of the company. I felt confident to let the managers manage. This not only made them happier and more effective, but it also freed up time for me to continue to improve the company and its culture.

Between more effective communication and management, the company culture was rebuilt resulting in a better trust with our employees. So much so that we honored one of the most requested benefits communicated through the 15/Five feedback. We now have a flexible work from home policy that our employees are thrilled to have. Essentially, although they are still required to work 40 hours a week, the only day our employees have to be in the office is Wednesday. Additionally, our managers have weekly one-on-one meetings with their direct reports to provide leadership and guidance.

Today, I am happy to say that our culture is at the best level it has ever been. Our turnover rate has decreased dramatically and I receive positive feedback from my employees weekly. The best compliment of all I now receive is when an employee tells me that they know I truly do care about them and that they feel valued.

About Mike Wylie

Mike Wylie founded Standing Dog Interactive, a digital marketing agency in 2005. Standing Dog was one of the Inc. 5000 fastest growing companies in North America three years in a row, 2010-2012. In addition to Standing Dog, Mike developed and launched ReviewAnalyst, a social media and reputation management application for the hospitality industry which was acquired in Sept. 2011 by TrustYou based out of Germany. Mike continues to sit on their board. Prior to Standing Dog, Mike was the Vice President of eCommerce for Wyndham International and the Senior Director of eBusiness for Hilton Hotels. Wylie has been named one of the 25 Most Extraordinary Sales and Marketing Minds in Hospitality and Travel by HSMAI and served as founding Co-Chair of the HSMAI Internet Marketing Committee.

Tips from Lion Leaders

Leadership Art & Science
David Thomas – Operations Officer
McDonald's Corporation

When I think about the concept of a Lion Leader it brings
to mind courage. All great leaders first learn how to follow-
just as young cubs do in the lion pride. We modeled this our
first year (Plebes) at West Point in our journey to become
leaders of courage and character to serve our nation with
distinction and honor. Leadership starts from within and is
a maturing process. Our values and cultural norms provide
the map of this journey as we mature as a leader. One of the
strongest techniques, as I have moved through this
maturing process, was adapting best practices from people
I wanted to emulate, and their best practices became part of
a tool box I integrated into my own style. We must seek out
the best to learn from, as they do not and did not become
successful great leaders by accident.

I helped pioneer the Stephen Covey 4 Imperatives of
Leadership program that outlines the characteristics of all
great leaders throughout history in a multitude of
disciplines. It all starts with trust, as no one can lead or have
relationships with followers without it. Secondly, you must
communicate your vision and direction with clarity, so all
members of the group you lead are aligned. Thirdly, you
must have a core system that everyone understands as to
how we operate together and respect each other. Lastly, you
must unleash talent- this is more of an issue today with

Millennials, as they expect you as the leader to "walk the talk!"

In my experience, Authentic Leaders do some very important things to engage their teams to get results. They understand the art of listening-active listening. They are humble and allow and expect all members of the team to be engaged with the task at hand. Authentic Leaders are not afraid to show vulnerability, and can apologize when they make mistakes. In addition, they are gifted in the art of Emotional Intelligence. I have found my biggest successes are rooted in showing empathy to the one's I lead, and walking in their shoes, so I truly understand the world or challenges through their eyes.

Great leaders ask the right questions and invite open dialogue to get the best answers. This also leads to real focus on solving problems as well as buy-in from all stakeholders. Great leaders are action oriented and create no excuse cultures to deliver results. In my master's program, we learned that in business, best cultures always win. There is a focus on people and people development coupled with strong expected norms of behavior, attitudes, and values.

As it relates to a Lion Leader, great leaders are not afraid to make the tough decisions and revel in being change agents. They take smart calculated risks to move the team or organization forward to achieve the goal. On top of that, they have the courage to do the right thing even if it may cause them harm, as their integrity is the one thing no one can take away from them. Great leaders also possess great strategic vision, and infuse that vision throughout the organization so there is clarity of purpose. Beyond that, these same principled leaders plan to win, and can adjust the plan as needed to reach their stated or agreed upon goals. Great leaders surround themselves with great leaders and the most talented people. They want and need to be challenged, and know the best and smartest relative to subject matter, help insure having the best outcomes and success. This was a hallmark of General David Petraeus. Intelligence and knowledge is critical for leaders to be successful. In today's environment it requires continuous learning as the world around us is changing rapidly. There's a certain kind of energy leaders possess that encourages people to follow them. Some do it boldly and some do it quietly, as the message is what drives engagement. I believe some people are innately more comfortable leading than others. However, leadership is still a journey and a learned maturing process that takes time, and forever is evolving as new information and techniques become available.

Leaders have the ability to influence others. This is a key component to achieving results, and the best know they must depend on the team and others to reach their goals. In my experience at West Point, I found the focus on "a sound body supports a sound mind" is critical to longevity and consistency of performance. Most great leaders need stamina, and having a foundation and program of physical fitness allows them to always be able to perform at their best.

Great leaders are innovative and seek new ways of doing things. For example, most truly embrace technology, as technology if used properly is an enabler of performance. Beyond that, they use technology to mine out data to better support achieving results, as their focus is on the things that allow them to reach agreed upon goals and objectives. Over time, I found as a leader that my belief system had to change, as our country and people have become more diverse and accepting of diversity. Our best teams are the ones that embrace the talents everyone can bring to completing the mission.

My final thoughts are that Leadership is both Art and Science. Anyone given the right situation can step into the role of leader. The story of David and Goliath illustrates this idea. However, true leaders are on a continuous path of learning and maturing to be the best leaders they can possibly be.

About David Thomas

David Thomas has over 25 years of experience in all areas of operations and marketing, primarily in service-oriented multi-site leadership environments. He is currently an Operations Officer with McDonald's Corp. Prior to his return to McDonald's, he was the Co-CEO at LCA-Vision/LasikPlus from 2009-2013 and also a Co-Founder of ALVA Labs, which holds a US and International patent in terahertz excitation used to identify Improvised Explosive Devices (IEDs). He is a graduate from the U.S. Military Academy at West Point with a B.S. in Engineering, and completed five years of active duty service in several leadership and command roles. Mr. Thomas also holds a Master's of Science degree in Business Leadership from Northeastern University in Boston, MA and is currently enrolled in a Harvard Business School program.

Tips from Lion Leaders

Building a Team
Kelly Dewey -Vice President of Operations
ZMC Hotels

Leadership is about building a team. I want only high performers on my team. To get this, I look for people who want to be held accountable and who have the guts to hold me accountable. I won't accept mediocrity on my team and I don't want people who want to be average either.

Building a team of winning people begins by hiring right. Among all of the other steps such as smart recruiting, I favor peer interviews. I believe that the people that are going to be working with the new recruits should give input on who they get to work with. They also can see things from a different perspective than I do. Allowing my top people in each department to do this, (top front desk agents, top sales people, etc.) lets them know that I believe in them and helps them grow in their jobs as well. Once we have the right new people in place, we have defined roles and responsibilities and job accountability is explained. I allow team members to have bad days and am supportive, however, it cannot be a way of life. Excuses are simply to be checked at the door. If team members run into challenges they can't overcome, they have the support of their team and me. We bring these challenges to our manager's meetings and put our heads together to come up with solutions.

Manager's meetings are the time and the place that most of our growing occurs. No one is allowed to come to the meeting without some sort of challenge or without something to add to help our team grow. We always leave the property for these meetings so we have a different setting, but more importantly, we aren't being interrupted by staff. Sometimes these meetings are heated and we disagree, however, whatever we come to as a resolution in the meeting is gospel and we implement it and all stand side by side when we walk out of the meeting. To the team members on site, they are to never know about the disagreements that happened during the meeting.

When and if we have a team member who isn't pulling their weight, I meet with them right away to see if there is some sort of breakdown. If someone is dealing with something like a divorce or an extended illness of a child or parent, I will work with them, but I need to know what's happening. I also can't allow things to drag on for too long for the sake of the rest of my team, so I'll offer alternatives to the teammate with challenges. If it is none of this and they are just in a funk, sometimes helping people realize the funk is enough, for others, it takes parting ways. Regardless, my actions everyday are determined by what is in the best interest of my team and what it takes to keep them functioning as the high-level performers they are. I tell everyone who is considering joining our team, we operate as gears in a watch, we all have to be turning at the same speed and in the same direction all the time or something will break. We can't have one department that is amazing and one that is just okay or those gears aren't moving at the same speed. We all have to support each other and we can only be the best, there is no other option.

To get a team of top level performers, you have to be authentic, transparent, and vulnerable as a leader and require the same from your team. These can all be difficult but for those willing to show their guts, and do it, you will build a team that has a high level of trust and can overcome almost anything together. Once your team sees you walking the talk every day, they will know that you mean business and will learn to love and respect you for it. They will also know that no one other than you will lead them into success and greatness. Share your vision and lead your team!

About Kelly Dewey

Kelly Dewey is a graduate from Northern Arizona University who has spent over 23 years in hospitality in Arizona with a background in sales and operations. Kelly and her husband enjoy traveling to visit their children who are grown and live out of state. Kelly also enjoys yoga and hiking.

Tips from Lion Leaders

In Support of Lion Leadership
Robert Ball – Chief Operations Officer
Atlas RFID Solutions

When I look back at my career in the military and business, there are a small handful of leaders that I would blindly follow to hell and back – and I'm confident we would find a way to win! I recall vividly the actions that set those leaders apart, which has served as a guide in shaping my leadership style. That is, (1) I genuinely believed they had my best interest at heart; (2) they created a shared vision of pushing the boundaries and accomplishing the impossible; and (3) they held the team to an uncompromising accountability of integrity.

As a young cadet at West Point, you are taught very early to put the needs of your soldiers before the needs of yourself. You are taught to eat last, sleep last, and to never ask a soldier to do something that you wouldn't first do yourself. If done genuinely, these simple actions create an unbreakable trust, which is critical when faced with difficult challenges especially during times of crisis. As a 27-year-old Captain in the Army, I took command of an M1A2 Abrams Tank Company in Baghdad, Iraq. Responsible for over 100 of America's finest, I knew I had to first earn the respect of my men. Respect is gained over time and is built on trust. On my first mission as a company commander, I decided to set the example by leading in the first vehicle of the combat patrol. It is important to understand that doctrine states the commander lead from the middle of the patrol to be in the best position for command and control while also reducing the risk of key leader casualties. At the time, the risk of roadside bombs where very real and if encountered it was almost always likely to strike the lead vehicle. It is the most dangerous position of the patrol. By leading from the front, I earned the trust of my men that I would not ask them to do anything that I was not first willing to do myself, especially when it involves personal sacrifice. I did not broadcast the reasons for why I chose to break doctrine. I wanted my men to come to that conclusion themselves, because it was honestly the truth! That one act did not fully engrain trust in and of itself, but through many similar acts, trust was formed. I was never questioned when giving commands on the battlefield – for the men knew I had their interests at heart.

In business, the most successful leaders inspire and empower others to push the boundaries of the impossible – to focus on "how we can" not "why we can't." I am reminded of a simple exercise that demonstrates this point by a CEO I classify as a Lion Leader. A consultant was brought in to help our team improve efficiency. Our team of 12 junior leaders were tasked to move as many tennis balls through a process within two minutes. The team was then given one minute to discuss ways to improve the process and iterate three times to see how much we could improve. The first results were less than 30, the second almost 50, and by the third attempt we achieved our goal of 100. At the end, the consulted stated, "What if I told you the record was 330?" Immediately the CEO stood up and said, "Let's go, we can beat that!" No-one on the team objected. There were no excuses. The team quickly worked together to think outside the box to focus on a solution. We found a way to achieve 384. To be clear, the CEO did not recommend the solution. The solution was identified by the junior leaders. The CEO had created an existing culture and common vision of being a "great company where good is not good enough." Whether it was a simple game or penetrating a new market, the team thrived on accomplishing the impossible through this shared vision of excellence.

Finally, let me discuss the importance of uncompromised accountability of integrity. When faced with failure and odds stacked against you, it is tempting to look for excuses to justify why the goal was not accomplished. For those who have the fortitude to persevere, it is also tempting to look for ways to cheat or otherwise compromise integrity for a short term gain. The most successful leaders will create a culture in which excuses and integrity violations are not an option. While working at a young startup company struggling with cash flow, we were at the point where we would likely need to lay off employees. Our CEO was presented a lucrative government funding opportunity that would solve our cash flow issues. While this opportunity was entirely legal, it was not within the spirit of which the government program was intended. The CEO brought the leadership team together and we discussed how we should proceed. We took a silent vote and unanimously the 5 senior company leaders all voted to reject the opportunity. More impressively, the team found other ways to honorably overcome our cash flow issues through hard work and determination. That event served as a rally point for the years to come. When faced with dozens of other challenges in growing a business, the employees rallied behind that event. They found the courage to always act with integrity and never give up – to accomplish the impossible.

About Robert Ball

Robert has 15 years of experience in project management and leadership responsibilities. Robert holds a Master of Business Administration from Duke University and a Bachelor of Science from the United States Military Academy at West Point. Robert is currently the Chief Operating Officer of Atlas RFID Solutions, responsible for operational excellence and accountability across Sales, Marketing, and Operations departments. Previously, Robert served as a Project Manager with The Shaw Group, responsible for delivering engineering, procurement, and construction scope to Client's within the Power Industry, managing projects in excess of $1.5 billion. Robert previously served as an Armor officer in the United States Army. He achieved the rank of Captain, leading over 100 soldiers in multiple combat tours in support of Operation Iraqi Freedom where he earned the Bronze Star Medal with Valor device for actions under enemy fire.

Tips from Lion Leaders

EPILOGUE

Throughout my life and career in business, I have always enjoyed being a leader, but I was not always in pursuit of becoming a Lion Leader. Mostly because I was my own biggest obstacle. I was often distracted by doing things my way or by people and things that kept me from stepping into my full potential. I knew there was a "bigger picture," I was just not focused enough to see it. I was an authoritative leader early in my career. I lead with a heavy hand and managed irresponsibly. As a result, I dealt with the repercussions through a lack of engagement and I decided to take action and improve. However, I only took action to improve, when I chose to be aware my ineffective skills and to seek out guidance from mentors. I came to understand the purpose of being an effective leader, and I became stronger than ever. Not in a controlling way, but in a humbled position of silent strength.

I have learned, through failure and success, that I must be healthy in three categories: spiritually, mentally and physically. These core life components will always be works in progress for me, however I am committed to my success. With regards to success, I have always felt that my purpose was to help others through the gift of words. I have always dreamed of becoming a professional speaker and trainer, but for the largest part of my life, I only considered this a dream. Who was I to accomplish this?

This was a negative thought that I burdened myself with. So, who am I? I am a son of our King. I know Him and He knows me. Today, all because of Him, and through my obedience, I am living my life's dream, my life's goal and most importantly, my life's purpose.

Believe in God. Accept Him and His plan for your life. Have faith and take action. You too can become a Lion Leader.

Lion Leadership

Lion Leadership

About The Author

Mike Rodriguez is CEO of Mike Rodriguez International, a global speaking and training firm. Mike is a multi-Best Selling author, with many of his books featured at Barnes & Noble book events. He is a world-renowned motivator and a leadership and sales expert. Mike has co-hosted trainings alongside the legendary Tom Hopkins and he is a former showcase speaker with the world famous Zig Ziglar Corporation. In fact, Mike was selected as the featured speaker and sales expert for their 2015 Ziglar U.S. Tour.

Mike has been featured on CBS, U.S. News & World Report, Fast Company and Success Magazine. He has lectured at Baylor University, UNT and K-State Research. His clients include names like Hilton, McDonalds's Corporation and the Federal Government. As a master trainer, Mike has worked with thousands around the globe.

He is a high-energy leader who worked in corporate America for over two decades training, building, mentoring, and developing top performing people and teams. Mike started as a struggling sales representative, with no experience or formal training. He worked his way up to become a top-performer and an award-winning sales leader. He credits his faith, having a plan, taking action, and never giving up for enabling him to prevail over many failures and adversities in his own life. Most importantly, he has always believed in his God-given potential.

Throughout his career, Mike has built productivity-driven training programs and managed multi-million dollar quotas. He has experience delivering powerful messages and creating personal development strategies for new and tenured companies and teams across many industries.

He believes if you have the right attitude, you can have the right kind of success, regardless of the type of industry that you. Mike has been happily married since 1991 to the love of his life, and together they have five beautiful daughters. are in.

As a world-renowned speaker,
Mike has experience working with people
from all backgrounds, personally and professionally.

You can schedule Mike Rodriguez
to speak or train at your next event.
Go to:
www.MikeRodriguezInternational.com

Other books available by Mike Rodriguez:

Finding Your WHY
8 Keys to Exceptional Selling
Break Your Routines to Fix Your Life
Think BIG Motivational Quotes
Walking with Faith
Life Builders
The Book on Selling

Audio Courses (MP3/CD) Available in December 2016 from:
Nightingale Conant

Lion Leadership

Disclaimer & Copyright Information

Lion Leadership

I can do ALL THINGS through Christ
who strengthens me.
Philippians 4:13

Lion Leadership

...........now go forth and become a Lion Leader.

Lion Leadership

CPSIA information can be obtained
at www.ICGtesting.com
Printed in the USA
LVOW04*0714081216
516366LV00006B/24/P